WANTED:
A
RULE BREAKER

Rules broken by
highly successful people

***Part* 2**

K.B. ROMAN

ROMAN WORLD PRESS

Published by: Roman World Press
PO Box 7 ABG, Sebele
Gaborone, Botswana
Email: kbromanworldpress@gmail.com
Fb/romanworldpress
+267-77 999 041

K.B. Roman
Email: kbromanbooks@gmail.com
Facebook page: K.B. ROMAN
+267-77 999 041

To God Almighty, for inspiring this work and faithfully seeing it through to completion.

To each reader.

To each Person who contributed to the success of this book.

CONTENTS

ABOUT THE AUTHOR

K.B. Roman is a Scriptwriter/ Screenplay writer, speaker, entrepreneur and an author of 18 books. Roman address different subjects, but the focus is on true identity, purpose, leadership and potential discovery and maximization, which leads to a true sense of purpose, meaning and fulfilment out of life.

INTROUCTION

I **wrote this kind of a book because I was** given rules that disadvantaged me in every way. **So many of them!** These rules have been accepted and embraced as a universal human culture and philosophy.

These are some of the rules… You are only human... You can't become it… You can't do it… Become what everyone is becoming… You are not the right person, material or type… You don't have what it takes… It hasn't been done before... Do what everyone is doing… This is how things are done.

Some people made these limiting rules. Someone must break them to make a way for rules that encourage and support true success, greatness and fulfilment. Highly effective, successful and great people break these limiting rules to become, do and achieve what they want.

These rules are enemies of humanity, true success, greatness and a sense of fulfilment. They produce indecisive average people, fence riders or people who live between lives and opinions. They produce human clones, carbon copies, imitations and scarecrows.

They produce people who spend a lifetime as visitors, refugees and illegal immigrants in a domain that is rightfully theirs. They produce receivers, spectators, fans and disciples of fellow human beings.

There are so many **cants** overpowering **cans** in this world. This book corrects these errors. This book raises a generation of rule breakers: risk takers, barrier breakers, line crossers, pace and record breakers and setters, situation and world changers, history changers, makers and directors.

And finally… the **three** most important rules you should observe without fail.

- Never place limiting rules on yourself.
- Never allow anyone to place limiting rules on you.
- Never place limiting rules on other people.

Happy reading! ☺

1

YOU DON'T HAVE WHAT IT TAKES

You don't have what it takes. You can't become, do or achieve it. You are unable to become, do or achieve it. You shouldn't become or do it. Don't become it. Don't do it. Don't even think about it. Don't even try.

You don't have what it takes to become, do or achieve it, this, that or what you want. You don't have what it takes to fulfil that dream. You simply don't have what it takes.

People will tell you that you can't or won't be successful in becoming, doing or achieving what you want because they think or believe you don't have what it takes to become, do or achieve it. They will tell you that you are not the right person, material or type to become, do or achieve what you want.

You are not the right person to be successful in these. You will not make it in a situation like that. Some people tried but didn't make it, and so will you. You are not any better than them. You are human like them.

I hear your point but the truth is that you won't make it because you don't have what it takes. Forget it and try something else. I see that as your way of inviting problems to yourself. You are placing yourself out there for frustration, disappointment and embarrassment. I wouldn't even try that if I were you.

The question is, who said I don't have what it takes to become, do or achieve what I want? Who said I can't or I won't make it? Who said I am not the right person? How do they know? How do they know the right person? How does the right person look like?

This doesn't make sense. It's unfair. It doesn't even sound right. What makes them to think that I don't have what it takes when I know I have what it takes: I am not the right person when I know I am the right person?

What makes them to think that I can't or won't make it when I know I can make it and I will make it? Who said I will fail because other people failed in this thing or a similar thing? **I am not those people. Their failure doesn't determine my failure or outcome.**

The truth is that, no one knows or understands you and your abilities completely. You shouldn't consider their limiting rules. Dare to break these rules. Tell them you can make it if they say you can't make it. Tell them you will make it if they say you won't make it. Break their rules and make your own rules.

Reject what they believe about you and follow what you believe about yourself. You have the right to choose to become or do what you want. No one has the right to place limiting rules on you. This is your life. You are not the people who failed. You don't even know why they failed. Refuse to listen to these kinds of rules.

How do they know you can't or won't make it? Who told them you can't or won't make it? Where is it written that you can't or won't make it? **You can make it. You will make it. You should make it.** Where is it written in the Bible that people's failures are determined by other people's failures? This is unfair.

People should be given a chance to try what they want to do or believe they can do. We can't just look at people's outward appearance, backgrounds and situations and conclude that they can't or won't make it: they can't or won't be a success in what they want to become, do or achieve.

Go for what you want to do if you believe or know you want to do it or can do it. It doesn't matter whether you fail in doing this thing. Failure is not even as bad as we see it.

Sometimes we call a platform for gaining valuable experiences and lessons "failure" because of ignorance.

It's better to fail than to stay away from trying. Trying something provides a foundation where you can build something. But where and how do you build without a foundation?

When we try to do things we gain valuable experiences and lessons that we couldn't get otherwise. We discover our abilities and strengths when we try or do something.

You tell people that you want to become a particular thing and they tell you that you can't make it and you won't make it in becoming that. So, don't even try it. You tell them you want to do a certain course or business and they tell you it is difficult, and so, you can't make it and you won't make it. So, don't do it. Don't even try it.

They will tell you about some people who tried that and failed. They just can't understand that you are not these people and that you may make it through where these people failed. How can people tell you that you are not capable when you know or tell them you are capable?

We don't just say things randomly without thinking. If you hear someone saying they want to do a particular thing you should understand they thought through it.

We are not saying you can't advise people on the decisions they want to make. **Advising someone and despising someone are two different things.** Does it make sense for someone to tell you, I am strong in this area and you tell them they are weak in that area: I am able to do it and you tell them they are not able to do it? Does this make sense? Is this fair?

I can become this and you tell them they can't become it; I have what it takes and you tell them they don't have what it takes? What do you want them to do? *Kill themselves?* **This is witchcraft.**

You tell people you want to start a particular thing and they tell you that you don't have what it takes. You won't make it. You will quit along the way. *Are they your directors?* We shouldn't listen to these kinds of people.

A person tells you they want to get married and you tell them marriage is hard and that they can't do it and won't make it. They are unable to handle the challenges of marriage. **They are not the marriage material or type.**

Who told you this? What makes you believe they are not the marriage material or type? What is marriage material or type? How do you know those who are destined for marriage and those who are not?

How do you know or determine the marriage material and type when people are not written these on their foreheads, chests or backs?

This one is a marriage material and type. This one is not a marriage material and type. *This doesn't even sound right.* **Who said marriage is for saints or perfect people?** Some people have good marriages amid the weaknesses they have in other areas. Some people are making it in business amid the weaknesses they have in other areas.

No one has reached the end of all perfect. We are a work in progress. We learn daily to improve ourselves.

Someone says they want to get into films and you tell them they can't and they shouldn't because they don't have what it takes. How do you know? What makes you believe they can't or won't be successful? What if they are one of those who are meant to be successful in this field?

You tell people that you want to get into business

and they tell you that you won't make it because you don't have money. Are we saying that all the successful business people had lots of money when they started their businesses? Anything can be done or achieved. We can't stop people from doing and achieving what they want because we believe they don't have what it takes.

We just can't get it somewhere from our heads and be convinced that someone can't do what they say they can do. You can't do that because you don't look like the people who normally do it. You don't have the perfect body. You don't have relevant abilities. Says who? So what?

Someone read my books and told me to my face that the content in these books doesn't suit me. There are two reasons that made him to say this. **My outward appearance and the way I handled myself.**

According to him, I was too calm, relaxed, collected and humble even with this kind of content or achievement. I don't know what he wanted me to do or how he wanted me to behave.

The truth is, I can't start jumping around as if I don't know or understand who I am: as if my intelligence or content is a surprise to me; as if I achieved these by accident, mistake or coincidence.

I can't start walking all over people's heads

because I have this great content. This is a part of me that doesn't go up to my head.

How can I go around acting as if I have become all and the best I should be: done all and the best I should do; achieved all and the best I should achieve?

People who have discovered themselves: who understand who they really are; who understand what they have inside them; who understand what they should do, achieve and give during their lifetime are not arrogant. They can't be arrogant. They have no time for this.

They are too busy to entertain pride and arrogance. They are too focused on today and the future to focus on the past or past achievements.

They are too focused on achieving their dream success to focus on their current achievement.

They don't boast about their current achievements. They can be grateful for what they have done or achieved but they can't have arrogance. **What they should achieve is more than what they have achieved.** They haven't reached their destination yet, so there is no room for pride, arrogance or boasting

He believed that my outward appearance didn't look like it could contain the mind that could come up with great content.

He matched up my physical appearance with the content in my books.

He matched up my outward appearance with my inner ability or wealth.

This is the highest level of ignorance and ignorance manifesting at its worst. This is a tragedy!

People forget that our bodies are just physical structures that house the real person living inside us. This is a huge mistake and error that should be corrected with an immediate effect. Anyway, let's continue.

Many people went to the cemetery with their brilliant initiatives, inventions, creations and wealth because someone told them they didn't have what it took to be successful in working on these.

Someone told them they couldn't make it and were not able to do what they said they wanted to do. Some people abandoned their great dreams or brilliant ideas because those close to them told them they couldn't make it in what they wanted to do. Their loved ones told them they didn't have what it took to do or achieve what they wanted.

Some people live empty, miserable and unfulfilling lives because they were discouraged from fulfilling their true purpose for existence. They were made to settle into what they didn't want; into other people's opinions and ideas. In Part 1 of this book, I shared the three important rules that each of us should observe without fail.

1. *You should never place any limiting rule on yourself.*
2. *You should never allow anyone to place any limiting rule on you.*
3. *You should never place any limiting rule on anyone.*

The Hard Truth

This is the hard truth that we should learn to live with.

- We shouldn't impose what we believe or our rules on other people.
- If you know you don't have what it takes to do a particular thing, don't assume everyone is like you.
- Don't assume everyone has your weaknesses.
- Don't determine people's abilities, outcomes and destinies by yours.
- Don't put everyone inside the box you have put yourself into.
- Don't paint everyone you see with the same brush

and paint you use on yourself.

- Don't assume everyone is a failure or will fail because you see yourself as a failure or have failed.
- We are different and unique. We have different abilities, strengths, weaknesses, sources and motivations.
- Some people have what you don't have.
- They can become, do and achieve what you can't.
- They will become, do and achieve what you won't.
- They want to become, do and achieve what you don't want.
- They may become, do and achieve what you may not.
- They should become, do and achieve what you shouldn't.
- They are meant to become, do and achieve what you are not meant to become, do and achieve.

So, we should learn to leave people alone or let them be; let them become, do or achieve what they want. We should learn to give people a chance to do what they want, even if they fail in what they do.

Failing is not the end of life, the world or

everything. It's just another bump on the road that we can pass.

Many people were told that they were unable to become or do certain things. They broke these rules and did what they wanted. They became a success in what they wanted to do because they became rule breakers. We shouldn't listen to these limiting rules placed on us. These are enemies of our progress, success and destiny.

You should be very careful. **A human being is the trickiest being on this planet.** The same people who tell you that you can't achieve the success you want, will come back to you and say things when you achieve your dream success because of breaking their rules. They will come and congratulate you. They will tell you that they always knew from the beginning that you will be successful.

Many people were told that they were not able to do certain things they wanted to do. Some people told others that they wanted to be pilots, astronauts or doctors. They were told to their faces that they couldn't and wouldn't become these because they didn't have what it took to become these.

There is what is known as education, learning and training. How do you even judge someone before they go for training? These people were told that they didn't stand a chance in what they wanted, and therefore should try something different or easier.

Some were given these limiting rules or were told that they didn't have what it took because what they wanted to do was associated with a certain class of people.

They were reminded of their disadvantaged backgrounds; the families they came from. They were reminded that their parent's names were not known.

They were told that they didn't have the right connections with the right people. What they wanted to do was not meant for them but for certain people's children. They should come from certain backgrounds, families or places for them to become or do what they wanted.

Some people were told that they didn't have the voice or eloquent voices needed to do what they wanted to do. But they became successful because they didn't listen to these limiting rules. They broke these rules.

Sometimes it doesn't need someone to have the same thing everyone has to be a success. Sometimes uniqueness is what is needed for us to achieve our dream success.

Some people were considered for certain positions because of their uniqueness in a particular thing. Interviewers considered them even when they initially knew the kind of a person they wanted for the position.

We can't put everyone in one box. The world needs diversity brought about by our uniqueness as individuals. People are tired of the same thing being done the same way over and over again. They are looking for something different, unique, fresh and interesting.

We can't say this radio station should only employ workers who sound like the first workers who started with this station. Listeners will get bored to the core. We can't say television stations should continue hiring people who look and sound the same.

We can't invite people to come to our auditions and expect to get from them what we got from our former presenter. Competency and uniqueness should be considered.

If we still want the former presenter, why couldn't we do all we could do to keep him or her? Why can't we do all we can to get him or her back? How can we expect to get this particular person from other people? Why do we want to turn everyone into this one particular person?

> *We can't keep ruling people out because they are different from those we have always had: they do a different thing from what has always been done; they do things differently from how*

they have always been done.

This is not fair to people who have something unique to offer. We can't all be placed in one container and be forced to wear one size fits all. Why should all of us be expected to follow the same routine, procedure and process? We should break some of these, especially when they are ineffective, irrelevant or they don't work for us.

You can't make it in that if you do things that way: if you don't do things this way. *How do they know?* You can make it, you will make it and you should make it. You just need to be convinced that you want it: you want to make it; you can make it; you will make it; you should make it.

We shouldn't allow anyone to tell us that we don't have what it takes to do what we want especially when we know we have what it takes to do it. We shouldn't allow anyone to tell us that we can't and are unable to do what we want especially when we know beyond knowing that we can do it and are able to do it.

The methods and rules we observe were introduced by some people. **Why can't we be allowed to introduce our way of doing things?** We should be strong, courageous and stubborn enough to pursue what we want.

We can't just come into this world and live to obey

every rule. We should learn to live to break all the limiting rules. Pledge to be a rule breaker. Dare to be a rule breaker.

2

IT HASN'T BEEN DONE BEFORE

You can't do that, you shouldn't do that, and you won't be able to do that because it hasn't been done before. No one has done it before. No one is doing it. No one in your family, among your friends, in our neighbourhood, community or nation has done it or is doing it. We don't know of anyone who has done it or is doing it. We just don't see you being successful in that because it hasn't been done before.

The question is, so what if it hasn't been done before? What if I should be the first one to do it? What if I am the one who is meant to do it? What if I want to do it because I am the only one who has thought of doing it: who has confidence in his or her ability to do it successfully? What if this is the main reason for my creation and existence?

What is wrong in doing something that hasn't been done before? What is wrong in doing something for the first time? What is wrong with me being the first person to do it in my family, neighbourhood, community, nation or the world?

My understanding is that everything has its beginning. There is nothing that doesn't have a beginning except God, the Creator of the entire creation.

The Word of God in the Holy Bible says this about Him. He is the first and the last. The beginning and the ending. He is ancient of days. He is from everlasting to everlasting.

All these mean that He has no beginning or end. He has always been in existence. There was never a time that He didn't exist. There will never be a time that He won't exist.

He didn't begin with time because He began the time. What we call the beginning isn't the beginning. What we call the end isn't the end. He saw the beginning of the beginning and He will live to see the end of what we call the end.

All we are saying is that everything has its

beginning. The earth wasn't always there. God initiated its existence. All the natural living and none living things we see around us were once not here.

There are manmade creations around us. These were not there in the beginning. Someone initiated them and this is how they came onto existence. Imagine if the people who made these didn't make them because no one made them before.

There were no airplanes in the beginning. Someone created them even when no one had created them before. There were no tall buildings in the beginning. Someone initiated them even when they had not seen them before.

Look at everything we have around us: bridges, roads, vehicles, malls, houses, schools, hospitals and other things. There was a time these were not there. Some people did these even when they didn't exist before.

Look at the organizations we have around us. Look at the kinds of sports we have. Look at all the clothes we have. These were not there in the beginning. We can't exhaust all these, but what we are saying is that these things didn't exist before. Someone brought these into existence.

What is there to gain in settling for what has always been done or is being done? **Why should we live to only meet the needs that have been met**

already or are being met? What is wrong in doing new or different things? This diversity is good for humanity as it meets needs that haven't been met or are not being met. It balances and completes humanity.

> You need to be very careful. Some people don't know what they can do with a wealth of limiting rules they have been accumulating in their heads since birth.
>
> They will go around imposing these on anyone and everyone. You will be their target if you look like you don't have a stand on anything or have nothing to stand up for.

These rules can be found everywhere. People will tell you that your business idea won't work because it hasn't been done before and that no one is currently doing it. I have seen financial institutions rejecting viable business ideas simply because they were new ideas.

They don't know if these will be successful because they haven't seen anyone doing businesses of this kind: they haven't funded business ideas of this kind before. So, they will not fund any business of this kind.

Some families clip their children's feathers and cage then by saying they shouldn't do what hasn't been done in the family. They shouldn't do what no one is doing as they will fail in it.

There is no guarantee that people will fail in what they do simply because it hasn't been done before. There is no guarantee that people will be successful in what they do simply because it has been done before.

You can't do that because we don't do that in our family. No one in this family has done or is doing what you want to do. Forget that and do something else. Do what everyone is doing in this family.

You can't be in politics because no one in this family has done it before. No one with your background has won this constituency before. Forget it and save yourself from frustration and embarrassment.

You can't desire to be the president of this country. You can't make it. I wouldn't even think about it if I were you. No one from our tribe or region has even tried that. Try something else. You don't stand a chance.

No one in our family has been in business before. So, you can't do it. You won't make it. Don't do it. Why can't you do what is being done by everyone? Why can't you look for a job like all of us? Your life will be secure.

As a different thinker and a rule breaker, just this one passage of these limiting rules above makes terrible unbearable noise to me. **This is one of the worst tortures to the human mind.** This is how people feel every time we place negative limiting and destructive rules on them.

These words are unbearable and this is the reason most of the people we say these words to will easily quit. They quit because they don't want to experience this mind torture from you again if it happens that they fail in what you said they will fail in. They don't want to hear one of the worst expressions. *I told you.* I you were going to fail.

It doesn't mean that everyone who does what hasn't been done before will fail. On the other hand, it's common to fail when you do something for the first time. There is nothing wrong in this. This is not new or strange. This is not the end of everything. They are not beyond redemption. They can do it again if they want.

Think of the amount of time medical experts spend on finding cures for diseases. They spend many years researching and experimenting.

Experts have been working for many years and are still working to find the cure for cancer. Will it make sense for us to tell them to stop trying because the cure they are trying to come up with hasn't been discovered before?

Should they stop because they are doing what no

one has done before? Should they quit or kill themselves because they failed many times?

They failed many times and there is nothing wrong in this. Without these failed attempts they have no foundation to work on. These failed attempts work as a foundation for the right cure.

What we call failure is a platform for getting valuable experiences and lessons that will help us achieve success in our next attempt.

We shouldn't quit at the first sign of failure. You can fail in your first attempt because you haven't been on this journey before. There is no one with the relevant experience to guide you in what hasn't been done before. It's okay to make some mistakes in the process.

People should be allowed to make some mistake or fail. This is not the end of everything. People shouldn't be judged brutally when they encounter what everyone calls failure because they tried to do something that hasn't been done before.

You have never been married before. This is your first marriage. You are likely to encounter some challenges and make some mistakes. You will learn some things while going through this marriage.

You don't need to have done something before or many times to be successful in it. Some people have been in so many relationships but they can't be successful in any of their relationships. Some people married several times and divorced. Some married many wives. These don't guarantee success in marriage.

Life is a journey. We keep gaining lessons throughout this journey. **You will meet challenges in life regardless of how smart you are.** You will meet challenge in your business even with that best business plan and great employees.

You have never been a parent before so you shouldn't judge yourself cruelly when your parenting skills are challenged. You may fail in that business because this is your first journey. It's okay. You shouldn't allow the fear of failure to stop you from trying or doing what you want to do.

Fearful people can never become history makers. They can never make marks in their generations.

No risk-taking no return. It's better to try and fail than to live with the regret of not even trying.

Who died from doing something that hasn't been done before? We shouldn't observe limiting rules like these. We shouldn't enforce them on ourselves or other people.

Look at yourself. You reached and passed the different stages of your life for the very first time and you made it through. All your life you have been doing the things you never did before.

You went to primary school, secondary school and tertiary for the first time. Was there anything wrong? You never did these before but you managed to go through these and became a success.

There was a time you were starting your job for the very first time. You became successful. There was a time you drove a car for the very first time. Did you die or lose anything for doing this for the first time?

You took up the building project of your house for the first time and you completed the house. There was a time you were not married. You got married for the first time and you are still in this marriage. You never had children before. You had the first child and nothing was wrong in this.

You can't tell someone they can't go overseas for their studies or to stay there because no one in their family has done it. People from other families did this. **These are human beings like this human being you are destroying with your destructive rules.**

No one has done that course in this family or

community. So what? What if this person should be the first to do it? Many people are used to these limiting rules. They even place these rules on themselves.

Some people can't think of doing something without scrutinizing through things to check for negative things that will justify why they can't, won't and shouldn't do what they want to do.

These are people who can come up with a dream or idea and kill it before they give it a chance. They abort their dream or idea because no one has fulfilled this kind of a dream or idea before: because no one seems to be having or fulfilling the same or similar dream; because they haven't fulfilled this dream before.

Imagine if people who achieved greatness and made history allowed other people to stop them from doing what they wanted simply because what they wanted to do was never done before or didn't exist. The world is a better place because these history makers broke all the limiting rules placed on them.

We shouldn't abandon our brilliant ideas because something similar to it hasn't been done before. We shouldn't quit our dreams because we haven't worked on this kind of dreams before.

There is nothing wrong in doing something for the first time: in being the first person to do a particular thing. We should be very proud of ourselves every time we come up with something new: we do or achieve something new or different.

We can't live to do only what has been done or what is being done.

We can't live to meet the needs that have been met already or are being met.

Doing what has always been done or is being done is a sign that there is too much copying and pasting things from other people onto ourselves. This shows that some people have no vision for their lives. They wait for other people to come up with ideas for them to copy and paste onto themselves.

This denies us an opportunity to be creative. We can't always settle for what has always been done or is being done. Will you be proud of yourself? Will you get a true sense of purpose, meaning and fulfilment from using other people's intellectual property? You should learn to have faith and trust in your creative ability. Give your creativity a chance.

Imagine These

There is a problem with these limiting rules. They don't even sound right. Imagine telling Leonardo Da Vinci not to do all the creations he did because no one did them before. Imagine saying these to him.

Are you out of your mind Leonardo? Creating Monalisa is a bad idea because it doesn't exist. You can't do it because it hasn't been done before. You shouldn't do it because no one is doing it. You won't be successful in that because you are the first person to do it.

Imagine telling Bill Gates that Microsoft was a very bad idea because it didn't exist: because no one in the whole world did it or was doing it. Imagine telling Mark Zuckerberg not to start Facebook because no one started it: because it didn't exist before; because he was the first person to create Facebook.

Imagine telling the late former president of South Africa, Mr Nelson Mandela that he couldn't become the first black president of South Africa because there was never a black president before. Imagine saying this to him. Do you think you are smarter than all the black politicians in this country? You are human like them and I don't see you making it. I wouldn't try this if I were you.

Imagine saying this to Mr Barack Obama? You are wasting your time sir. I just don't see you making it. You can never be the president of the United States of America because there has never been a black president before. You won't make it because you are the first black person to do it. No one in your family has done that. I wouldn't even try it if I were you.

Imagine telling Mother Teresa not to help the people of Calcutta, India because no one from her family or country did it before or was doing it. I don't see you making it, especially that you are a female single foreigner.

Imagine telling the first person to fly an aircraft not to do so because no one did it before or was doing it. Imagine telling the person who initiated mobile phones not to go ahead with his idea because no one had produced mobile phones before.

Someone initiated light bulbs for the first time. Imagine telling him not to do so because bulbs didn't exist that time or before. Imagine the world without all these.

Our lives are better and comfortable because of these people who dared to break all the limiting rules placed on them.

How can we live to do only what has been done? Imagine how the world and our lives would be if we were to stop producing new things. We settle into doing old things that have always been done or are being done.

As a different thinker and a rule breaker, I pledge to break every rule that discourages me from exercising my originality and creativity. I will rebel against all the rules that say I shouldn't start new things: I shouldn't do different things; I should only settle for what has been done or is being done by everyone.

> I will do what I want, the way I want it and when I want it. No one and nothing will stop me from giving a chance to my originality and creativity by telling me that I shouldn't do things because they haven't been done. I pledge to be faithful to my rule breaking pledge.

3

DO WHAT EVERYONE IS DOING

People will tell you to do things because everyone is doing them. They will tell you not to do things because many people are not doing them. Normally when they say everyone they refer to family members, relatives, neighbours, friends, schoolmates and workmates. They refer to people in your community, nation or the world.

Why do you want to do that? *My answer- why shouldn't I do it? What's wrong with me wanting to do it?* Why do you want to do what other people are not doing? Why not do what everyone is doing? *My answer- because I am not them. I a me, myself and I- a different individual, separate and unique. Got it?*

Why do you want to differ from everyone? *My answer- why shouldn't I differ if I want to?* No one is doing that around us. *My answer- so what if they are not doing it?*

Is it my business if they choose not to do it?

You can't do that because many people are not doing that. You shouldn't do that because many people are not doing that. You won't make it in that because many people are not doing that. Do what everyone is doing and you will do just fine. *My answer- how do you know I will do fine?*

You should do this or that because everyone in this family is doing it. You shouldn't do this or that because no one in this family is doing it or has done it before. That has been the practice, tradition or culture of this family for many years. This is what this family does and is known for.

As a different thinker and a rule breaker, I can't help making faces and rolling my eyes right now. This comes to my mind when I hear the above statements. **This family, my foot! What about me as an individual?** *What about my practice, tradition and culture as an individual? What about what I want to be known for as an individual?*

Their rules continue. Why should you be different from other family members? Why should you do different things that are not done or haven't been done in this family?

Why should you do things differently from how we do them in this family? That will ruin the reputation of this family. What will other people say?

My answer- who are they anyway? And who cares what they say?

Why do you want to do a different course? No one is doing that or has done it in this family. We don't know of anyone who has done that in our neighbourhood or community? You should do this or that course because many people are doing it. Your cousin and friend are doing it. Our neighbour's child is doing it.

My answers- none of the above is my business. Why should it always be me doing their thing their way. Why can't you tell them to do my thing my way? You want me to be a nurse or an accountant like them? Why can't you tell them to be writers or filmmakers like me?

You see, there are always those who are being favoured. All of us should be like them. The truth is, not all of us are cut for these things. Not all of us exist to obey rules.

Some of us look at things differently; from a different standpoint or angle; with a different perspective. **We have learnt the art of looking to see; the art of listening to hear.**

As a result, we see and understand things differently. This makes us different thinkers. This different thinking makes us rule breakers. These make us different people.

Some of us are different thinkers and rule breakers. This makes us misfits. Contrarians. Triangle houses on oval foundations. Steve Jobs puts it this way- Round pegs in square holes. These names are not new or strange to us. We can't help it. We can't help ourselves.

We understand you may be very uncomfortable with who we are, how we see things, what we do and how we do things. It's perfectly okay with us. There is nothing wrong with you. We live in different worlds. That's all.

We were also very uncomfortable in the beginning when we realized that we were different from many people; when we realized that we were going to stray and create our own paths or travel different routes from those taken by most people, including those very close to us.

We were very uncomfortable when we realized that we were going to be misunderstood; we were going to look ridiculous and be called funny names.

We didn't celebrate when we realized that we were different thinkers which gave birth to the rule breakers in us. This is because we understood very well that our path was going to be too narrow and challenging.

It's not like we didn't try anything. We realized that we were oddballs, misfits and contrarians-triangle houses or designs but we forced to build ourselves on oval foundations because everyone around us was doing that.

Unfortunately, this didn't work out. Some of our parts continued to protrude and grow beyond these oval foundations. This is how we changed foundations; built relevant and suitable foundations for ourselves.

We realized we were contrarians, but we tried to follow everyone going to the east and we became so miserable along the journey. That's how we decided to go west.

We realized we were round pegs but we forced ourselves into square holes as they were the only ones around us. This is how we stopped trying to be like everyone; do what everyone was doing. This is how we discovered our suitable round holes.

We couldn't fit in and this is how we accepted that we were destined to be oddballs, contrarians and misfits. This is how we stopped trying to fit into anything and everything. This is why we are not afraid to do things that haven't been done or take paths that haven't been taken before.

You see, it's not like we didn't try at all. We tried many times and for many years. This is like destiny. We can't help it. And there is nothing anyone, *including you,* can do about this except to learn to live with it.

People place these limiting rules on you for you to become like them; like the people they know; like many people; like everyone else. They want to reduce you to the general identity and purpose that is being embraced by many people or everyone.

They want to repeal and replace you with other people. They want you to spend a lifetime living the life of other people. They want to deny you an opportunity of a lifetime.

Each of us has one life or lifetime that is precious and too short.

You can't afford to give these to another person. You can't come into this world to live the life of another person.

You can't afford to allow other people to live two lives: to live inside you; to live through you.

- You can't reject your true identity and purpose to embrace what belongs to other people.
- You shouldn't put your dreams, ideas and desires aside to follow those of other people.
- You shouldn't put your needs aside to follow the needs of other people.
- You shouldn't sacrifice your sense of purpose,

meaning and fulfilment for the sake of other people.

- You should please others at the expense of your life and fulfilment.

I have a serious problem with these limiting rules. I don't do things because everyone does them or because many people do them. I don't stop myself from doing what I want or what I should do because I am the only one doing that.

I am the kind that isn't afraid to differ from other people: to do a different thing from what everyone around me is doing. I am not afraid to stand out of the crowd. This is the life I have lived for many years or since I can't remember.

People always wondered what my problem was and why I couldn't settle for what everyone was doing around me. I have discovered my true identity, individuality and uniqueness. I am very okay with these.

I do things because I should do them, not because everyone is doing them.

I don't follow a certain fashion style simply because everyone is following it.

I wear things because they suit me best: because I am comfortable in them; because they support the life or lifestyle I live.

Many people go through unnecessary pressure because they want to do what everyone around them is doing. They want to fit in. They go to certain places not because they want to go there or should go there, but because many people go there or are expected to go there.

Some people are in terrible situations because they went to certain places they shouldn't have gone to. They went there because they wanted to fit in. They went because they were told that they were backwards if they didn't go there. They didn't want other people to see them as misfits.

As for me, I have accepted that I am a misfit to the core. ***Proudly a misfit and loving it!***

I have where I belong already. I don't live to squeeze myself into things I don't want or understand to get people's approval.

Some people became substance addicts because they did what everyone around them was doing. They were under pressure to do what everyone was doing. Some people are into unhealthy relationships not because they want to but because everyone is involved. They end up in trouble because they can't withstand pressures from other people.

They allowed themselves to fall into a pit with their eyes open simply because everyone was falling into this pit.

They knew this wasn't good for them but they had to destroy their lives because everyone around them was destroying their life. Is this how we should live our lives? This is a tragedy. *Did you come into this world to be a disciple of everyone?*

You shouldn't do things because everyone, the whole world or people around you do them. Do what you should do. Do the right thing.

Bear this in mind. You are not everyone. You are not the whole world. You are not exactly like everyone. You are you. You are a separate, different and unique individual. You have an exclusive life.

You are a member or part of the human race but you are an individual. You are a human being like other human beings but you are a separate unique human being.

You may be a part of the body that makes the human race, but you are also a single part with its specific identity and function.

Think of the human body. Each part is different and has a specific unique function. We make the human race in this same manner but we are separate, different and unique.

Each of us has a specific unique purpose to contribute to this body to diversify, balance, complete and fulfil the human race.

You may be a part of the forest, but you are a separate tree that contributes to making this forest.

You may be one of the oranges on this tree and may look the same or similar, but each orange is separate. Each of these oranges may end up being used by different people, in different places and for different purposes.

These limiting rules stop us from becoming what we should become or could become. They stop us from doing what we should do or could do. There are those things we can do but we can't do them because other people around us are not doing them.

We have the ability or discipline not to do certain things but we do them because everyone around us does them. We can control ourselves but we don't because everyone around us seems to be out of control. We can live in integrity but we don't because everyone around us lives anyhow.

We can work harder for better results but we don't do this because everyone around us is relaxing and taking things easy in the name of working smart.

We suffer from crowd mentality. We follow crowds everywhere. We end up following people going nowhere because we desperately want to do what everyone around us is doing.

We live average lives, do average things and achieve average results even when we can go beyond average, simply because everyone around us is a member of the cult of average people or a cult called "the rest". We desperately want to maintain our membership in these cults.

We know we won't be judged because everyone around us is embracing the average life. We allow ourselves to live inside this box of limited thinking because everyone has settled into it. We don't break out of limitations because people around us are comfortable with these.

We don't cross the lines that stop us from becoming, doing and achieving what we want even when we can. This is because no one around us is crossing these lines. We don't cross because we don't have line crossers around us to inspire us to cross.

We don't increase our pace in what we do even when we can, because everyone seems to be relaxing and taking things easy. We don't maximize our potential in what we do even when we can, because everyone is relaxing and taking things easy.

We waste our time in things of no importance, significance and value simply because everyone or most people are doing that. Look at how people use social media. They waste their valuable time, strength and life misusing social media because many people do it.

I am calling this a waste because a human being has a lot to do and achieve during his or her lifetime on earth. I am calling this a waste because other people use the time we waste on social media to build and develop their lives.

Some people work long hours in their offices to achieve their dream promotion while others misuse social media because everyone seems to be doing it.

Some people are busy working on making history and you are busy looking for something funny to post on social media.

Some people are busy writing powerful books and producing rare paintings during the time we waste on social media. Some people are busy reading and building themselves up, and we are busy doing what we believe is being done by everyone on social media.

I know what I am saying here. I was very shocked when I started promoting my books on social media. I noticed there were people from two far countries who were dedicated to sending strange insulting and annoying inboxes.

These were not from where I lived. It got to a point where I decided not to open these messages. This is what came to my mind every time I saw what they sent to me.

Some people are busy fulfilling the purpose of their creation and existence but others are busy posting and inboxing nude pictures of themselves or the people they don't know to me.

Some people are busy building mansions and buying private jets for themselves, and changing the world but others are busy inboxing nude pictures, pornography, their private parts or those of other people to me.

I am busy promoting my books to fulfil a part of the main reason I exist and to make money, but some people are busy inboxing strange and annoying stickers to me- private parts and people making love.

Some people are busy out there accumulating wealth and building their legacy but some people are busy posting people in the privacy of their bedrooms.

This is a tragedy. Identity crisis at its worst. A miserable business in indeed. A complete waste of life and a lifetime. A complete misuse of the grace to be alive.

I remembered what Dr Myles Munroe said. **The greatest tragedy in life is not death but life without a purpose.** I agree with this 100%.

People who don't know what they should do or have nothing to do can do anything. People who don't know who they are or who they should become can become anything. These lead to a miserable, empty unfulfilling life and death.

There is nothing funny or interesting in this. Some people may find this interesting or funny, but not all of us. *Annoyingly disgusting.* How do you do this?

Where do you get the time to record your naked self or search pornography stuff?

And where do you get the guts to send it to other people?

I take these things seriously because these result from identity and purpose crises. It's easy to become anything if you don't know your true identity: who you are or who you should be. It's easy to do anything if you don't know your true purpose or what you should do. These make you the world's dangerous person.

This is the reason I keep saying that the world's most dangerous people are those who haven't discovered their true identity and purpose. They can become or do anything.

I don't think the people who understand who they are and what they should do and achieve during their lifetime can waste their valuable life and time on sharing nude pictures of people doing their things in their bedrooms. Sometimes you should just sit and ask yourself certain questions.

- Is this it?
- Is this what I have settled for?
- Is posting or sharing pornography videos and nude pictures on social media the main reason for my creation and existence?
- Is this what compelled my creation and existence?
- Is this what my Creator had in mind when He thought of creating me?
- Is this what I live for?
- Is this my true purpose for existence?
- Is this what I was sent to do in this world?
- Is this the only or best thing I could come up with after searching deep within myself for the things I could do?
- Is sharing pornography videos and nude pictures what still compels my Creator to extend my lifetime in this world?
- Is my Creator pleased when He looks at me doing this?
- What do I want to achieve from doing this?
- How does this add value to my life?
- Am I becoming a better person by posting, sharing and promoting these?

- Does this contribute to my development, success and fulfilment as an individual?
- Is this what I always dreamt of becoming and doing when I was growing up?
- Is this my ideal self, work and success?
- Am I being the best version of myself by doing this?
- Am I being all and the best I should be; doing all and the best I should do; giving all and the best I was sent to give to this world?
- Is this the best I can do with my life, time and strength?
- How does this add value to the people I send these things to?
- Is this my best contribution to humanity and our world?
- How does this make the world a better place?
- Is this what I want to be known for or be remembered for?
- Am I proud of myself and what I do?
- Will my parents, family or loved ones be proud of me when they see me doing these?
- Do I get a true sense of purpose, meaning and fulfilment from doing this?

The discovery of your true identity and purpose comes with a sense of responsibility and accountability to a particular thing and even in living your life.

People feel right and justified to do these because they believe they are doing what everyone around them or in social media is doing. This is what we are saying here.

You can't useless yourself because other people and the whole world are doing so. You can't waste your life, strength and time doing useless things because people around you are doing so. **Are you these people? Are you everyone? Are you the whole world?**

Who are you and what do you want as an individual? What would you do if other people were not doing these things? Were you sent to this world to be a disciple of fellow human beings? Do you exist to copy and paste other people and what they do onto yourself?

I am reminded of one of the best things I learnt while studying to be a screenplay writer. We were taught that we shouldn't just include anything we want in our scripts or screenplays. **Whatever we include in a scene should move the story forward or make it better.**

Maybe we could understand if you did all these for

money, but there is nothing here. It's just a waste of life, time and strength. This is living to please the enemy of your life, progress, success and fulfilment. You are cooperating with your enemy because the mission of the enemy is to reduce your value for you to become useless in life.

You can't reduce your value and make yourself useless because some people are doing that. You are better than this. **You are a god- the god of the earth. You are the most important and treasured being on this planet.**

You can't live to be controlled by what you should control. You can choose to change the direction of your life. You can abandon this empty life for you to embrace the abundant life meant for you.

No one is being judged here. Someone should help the human race. We are the keepers of our fellow human beings. It's our responsibility to take care of each other by sharing the truth that can set them free from certain entanglements.

We are all human beings and we are not perfect or haven't reached perfection. No one is looking for this perfection from anyone. But we have the responsibility to live lives that make us better people: lives that give us a true sense of purpose, meaning and fulfilment out of life and what we do.

We should understand who we are. We are human

beings or made of flesh and blood, but we are more than these.

Being a human being means that we have two makeups. You are a god and a man at the same time. Man here refers to both the male man and the female man.

You are a spirit being living in a human form. You are a god living in a human form.

You are a spirit being or god that lives in a form that has some weaknesses.

This human body or flesh is not the part that encourages people to misuse social media, but the person living inside this body. This inner person is the main person. He does anything because he is experiencing terrible identity and purpose crises.

What we are saying here is very important. I have seen people making themselves of less use because people around them are doing that. I have seen people losing their precious lives unnecessarily in protests or strikes.

In some cases, they didn't have to participate but they did because everyone around them was participating. I have seen people burning buildings and destroying things because they wanted the government to create jobs for them or develop their cities.

In most cases, they don't do this because they want to or see a need to do this, but because they see everyone around them doing this. They fear how other people will look at them or what they will say. They desperately want to fit in. *Most of these people can't be successful in life.*

Other people are busy using this time to build and grow their lives, wealth and greatness but they are busy protesting in the streets because other people are protesting: because they have to do what other people do; because they want to be like everyone; because they want to please other people; because they want to fit in.

If they don't die in this protest they will remain behind and stay unsuccessful.

The next thing they will say is that some people are lucky. There is nothing like being lucky here. The people you consider lucky were able to withstand the pressure they had to do what everyone around them was doing.

You consider them lucky but they were working very hard while you were busy protesting and wasting your life, time and strength on things without guarantee.

There is no guarantee that you will get what you protest for from the government. They may promise to do what you want because they want you to stop protesting, but there is no guarantee they will do that. They will always give reasons why they can't do what you want.

What we are saying here is, please don't just do things because everyone around you is doing them. You shouldn't become anything and everything because everyone around you is becoming it. You shouldn't just do anything and everything because everyone around you is doing it.

Know and understand who you are: who you should be; who you want to be as an individual. This will help you to become just that.

Understand who you are not: who you shouldn't be; who you don't want to become. This way, you will not become who you don't want to be or shouldn't be unaware.

Know what you want to do and what you should do. This will help you to become just that.

Know what you don't want to do and what you shouldn't do. This way, you will not do what you don't want to do or shouldn't do unaware.

Analyze and weigh things before getting involved. They will say you are backward or you don't fit in but it's okay. You have where you fit already. If they can't accept you into their class because you refuse to degrade yourself or destroy your life, so be it.

> You were not sent to this world to be a disciple of every fellow human being. You are not a clone, carbon copy, imitation and resemblance of any human being. You have a life to live, an identity to embrace and a demanding purpose to fulfil.

Imagine how the world would be like if some people didn't break the rule that said everyone should do what everyone is doing or should do things the same way everyone does them.

Think of all the great achievers and history makers. They successfully defeated the pressure to become or do what everyone around them was becoming or doing. They did what they wanted to do. They did things their way.

Someone in your family, neighbourhood, community or nation became a success in a particular thing because he or she broke the rule that said everyone should do what everyone was doing.

Someone became a successful painter, author, musician, designer, farmer or beauty therapist because he or she disobeyed the rule that said everyone should become or do what everyone was becoming or doing.

Look around you. We benefit a lot from the things that were done by people who were discouraged from doing them: people who were told to become or do what everyone around them was becoming or doing.

These people became successful because they didn't allow anyone to place limiting rules on them. They did what they wanted to do not what other people wanted them to do.

I wouldn't be a writer or author if I didn't break the rule that said I should become or do what everyone in my family, relatives, neighbours or community was becoming or doing. I wouldn't be an entrepreneur if I didn't break the rule that said I should take the employee route that everyone around me was taking.

I wouldn't have crossed certain barriers if I didn't break the limiting rules placed on me: if I didn't break the rules that were obeyed by those around me. I believe I became a successful rule breaker.

I became successful in breaking these rules because I didn't become what people around me were becoming. What I do is different from what they do. I don't know of anyone among them who travelled the path I travelled: who has been through what I have been through; who does what I do right now.

I refused to be placed in the same box that everyone in my family, friends, relatives or community were placed into by these limiting rule. I didn't want to see myself anywhere near this box.

They will label you for the life or path you choose to embrace. They will make you feel uncomfortable for doing what you want to do and for doing things your way. They will say you have a higher opinion of yourself.

You see yourself being higher than the highest. You think you are smarter and better than other people around you. You reach a point where even your family members or those close to you don't understand you.

Different thinking gives birth to rule breaking. You break these rules because you think differently. You understand things differently. **It's not easy to be a rule breaker and to live as a courageous rule breaker.**

Though this book, I encourage you to break all the rules that limit or affect your life, progress, success and fulfilment. Dare to break all these rules fearlessly, unapologetically and proudly. It's okay to be different from other people. This is how things are meant to be.

It's okay to do a different thing from what everyone around you is doing. It's okay to do things differently or your way. It's very okay to break limiting rules: to make the rules that work for you.

You were not sent to this world to obey every rule from every human being. These rules were made by other human beings. You are also a human being and can make the rules that work for you.

I am on a mission to raise a generation of rule breakers through this book. Each of us can become a rule breaker. We can make relevant rules that work for us.

THIS IS HOW THINGS ARE DONE

People don't only have problems with us doing different things from those done by everyone around us. They also have problems when we do things differently from how they are being done around us. This means that if we do what everyone around us is doing we should also do it the same way everyone is doing it or the same way it has always been done.

You can't do things differently here. You can't do it this or that way. Don't do it this or that way. Do it this or that way. This is how things are done here. This is not how we do things here. Everyone is doing it this or that way. It has always been done this or that way. We obey these rules every day.

This is how we do things or how we have been doing things in this family, company, organization, government or country. Things should be done and maintained this way.

You can't live differently or do things differently from how they are done here, otherwise you will have problems. You won be accepted here. You won't fit in here.

Most times we limit ourselves by embracing other people's lives and ways of doing things. **Everyone should fry fish and potatoes because everyone is frying them.** This is how we cook or eat in this family.

We can't learn new things because we are faithful to obeying the rule that says we should do things the way they are being done around us or the way they have always been done.

It is said that insanity is doing the same thing again and again but expecting different results. We do the same thing the same way and we expect different results from what we have been getting. Things don't work this way. Everyone should do the same business the same way.

Everyone is expected to study in his or her country. People will start questioning if you want to study abroad. They don't understand why you don't study locally like everyone else in your family, neighbourhood or community.

People will highlight all the challenges you will or are likely to meet in doing things differently. They will pressurize you to follow certain methods that don't even work for you.

They will question your intention to get married to someone from a different background, profession, culture, nation or race. Why should you marry differently? We are expected to run our marriages, families and homes the way other people around us run theirs. We are expected to get married around the same age.

We are expected to marry people with the same or similar background like ours: people who look the same or similar to those married by our parents, siblings or friends.

We are expected to get married the same way and for the same reasons. Marriages are breaking up because people are pressurized to follow patterns that don't work for them.

Why can't you do things the way other people do them? Why can't you do things the way your friends, siblings or people from other families do them? There is this common saying. I also want to this or that so that I become like other people or people from other families. I also want to do things this or that for me to be like other people.

I also want to dress this or that way because this is

how most people dress these days. I want to talk a certain way because this is how people talk these days. I want to do things the way everyone does them.

I have a serious problem with people who want all the members of the human race to do the same thing, the same way, and for the same reason.

I have met people who don't understand the writing career or field a bit. I am using writing as an example because this is what I understand better. Relate this to your field.

People will tell you what you should write and how you should write it. They will tell you that this is what every writer or most writers are writing *these days*. This is how they write *these days*.

Change to this genre because writers in this genre make lots of money. Write the way other writers write and you will be successful. Research about all the successful authors and write exactly the way they do.

I don't rubbish all these but writing the way everyone writes doesn't guarantee success. There is no guarantee that you will also become a bestseller.

What we fail to understand is that most of these authors become bestsellers because they embrace their unique content and writing style. There is power in embracing and maximizing your uniqueness as a writer.

People told me that my books won't be bought and that I should maybe consider writing on real estate. **My question was, what will I write on real state?** I have no idea.

You don't just wake up one morning and write on real estate because people make lots of money from this. Maybe in the future if at all something changes, but as for now I have nothing to write on real estate.

Being a writer doesn't mean that you should or will write on anything and everything.

Being a pilot doesn't mean that you will fly any aircraft. There are pilots who will never fly war jets. There are medical doctors who will never do a heart or bone surgery. There is nothing anyone, including you, can do about this. We can't despise these doctors or pilots because they specialize in a certain area.

We can't expect every architect or builder to build the Taj Mahal because this building is a wonder. We can't expect all farmers to produce all kinds of food in their farms. We can't expect all teachers to teach Physics or English language. Some will spend a lifetime teaching Accounts or Hindi language. And that's perfectly okay.

We will be so disappointed and frustrated to the core if we turn every human being into a jack of all trades and master of none.

We can't all do the same thing. Each of the things we do are like single puzzle pieces that each of us should contribute to the universal puzzle, to diversify, balance and complete humanity and our world.

There nonfiction writers who will never write fiction books. There are writers who will never write business, travel or spiritual books. And there is nothing wrong in this. We can't expect all writers to write horror novels or relationship books.

Some writers can't even put a short story together. Should all screenplay writers write romantic, horror or science fiction films? Imagine watching fifty movies from one genre for the whole year.

People will remind you that you are not writing for yourself but customers. This is true but some people don't even know the kind of books they need. Most people don't really know the kind of clothes they want. They will know when they see these.

A writer can reveal people's problems and ways of solving them or dealing with them. These are problems they may not even know they have. People may not know that they have identity confusion until they read a book about identifying and dealing with identity confusion. People may not know the kind of clothes they want but will know when they see them in shops.

People may not have a name for the challenge they are experiencing but may or will know when they see the answer or solution to this challenge.

We can't neglect other subjects to focus only on subjects that are being addressed by every writer or most writers. **Why should all of us live to meet the needs that are already being met or have been met?**

I can't always wait for other people to determine what I write and how I write it. I write what I am comfortable and confident with. I write what I can justify and defend when I am expected to.

We can't all write on real estate. We are given different messages to cater for different people, in different situations, with different needs. In most cases, writers write out of inspiration.

Each writer has a message they should share with humanity. Sharing this message brings a sense of purpose, meaning and fulfilment out of life.

The main reason for our writing or doing what we do is mainly inspired by the desire to fulfil our divine purpose on earth. Of course we can make money in the process of fulfilling our true purpose for existence.

I can do all I can to write on real estate with the help of other people and be successful, but I will not have the kind of fulfilment I get from addressing the subjects that I believe are connected to my true purpose.

I have discovered who I am and my message as an individual. I should share this message with the human race during my lifetime. If I am blessed enough my legacy should benefit next generations.

The central theme of my message is: True Identity and Purpose Discovery, Potential Maximization, and Attainment of a True Sense of Purpose, Meaning and Fulfilment out of life through what we do.

I exist to help individuals discover and embrace their true identity and purpose. I encourage people to be and do their best in everything for them to achieve a true sense of purpose, meaning and fulfilment from what they do and from life in general.

I can address different subjects, but I have realized that I always go back to my main message. I will use different means to share my message with the world. I will use books, films, television, internet, social media and other things to pass this message.

I can't write about computers or technology because many writers are writing on these. But my message applies in every area. When it comes to computers or technology, my part will be to encourage people to maximize their potential in their dealings with these. To encourage them to give their all and the best in what they do.

I may not be a farmer, but my message will encourage farmers to maximize their potential in their farming work until they achieve a sense of purpose, meaning and fulfilment from what they do. I may not be a nurse, but I will encourage them to give what they do their all and best. I hope you get my point.

As a rule breaker, I will not do things because everyone does them or they have always been done. I will not reduce myself to doing things a certain way because everyone or many people do them that way.

Think of the different singers or musicians we have around the world. Imagine the world with all singers singing the same way. We have different music because different people need different music. We can't all sing hip hop or jazz because many people around us are into that or we feel this is what everyone wants.

All filmmakers can't be pressurized to produce horror or science fiction movies because many filmmakers are producing these. Some great filmmakers will never do this kind of films but they have a sense of fulfilment in the kind they produce.

Many people don't know what they want until they

see it. We can't limit ourselves because of what people currently know or like. We do what we do best and people will like what we do.

All painters or artists can't be expected to do Monalisa or the last supper because these made Leonardo Da Vinci successful and famous. **He wasn't setting a pattern by doing these.** He did all he needed to do.

We are placing ourselves out there for disappointment and frustration if we try to do everything exactly the way others do it. People should be allowed to do what they want and what they feel they can do best. We can't expect people with different voices to sing the same way because many people are singing that way.

We can't all build the houses that are designed the same way. The whole neighbourhood will end up looking as if it belongs to one person or housing corporation. We can't all dress the same way as if the world has run out of design ideas.

We can't all be expected to speak the same way when our different voices reveal our Creator's plan to have people who speak differently. We can't be pressurized to do things the same way as if our Creator set this as a standard for the entire human race.

There are different ways of doing or achieving

things in life. We can't expect everyone to use the road when others can fly or sail. This is all we are saying. We can't all be pressurized to follow the same life pattern or lifestyle.

Each of us is a different and unique individual. Our lifestyles differ. Each of us is destined differently, and in most cases it's hard to go against this.

Everyone is expected to follow the same pattern of life. Everyone is expected to go through primary, secondary and tertiary schools the same way. From here, each of us is expected to look for employment and get a loan; buy a car and a house; get married and have children.

If you don't go through this process everyone will conclude that you have serious problems. **They will persecute you for messing up this pattern.** You will be persecuted for doing each of the above at an age that is not approved by everyone or society around you. You will not be given peace because you have not satisfied people's expectations for your life.

The truth is that this pattern doesn't work for everyone and it shouldn't. This pressure for everyone to do things a certain way has ended some people in serious problems. It has messed up or destroyed some people's lives and destinies.

Some people were pressurized to marry when they

were not ready simply because they had to do things the way everyone around them did them. Some were not ready for marriage but they were pressurized to marry for age. Some ended up leaving this marriage or family.

I see it as a very bad idea for me to do things a certain way because everyone around me does them that way or they have always been done that way. I will not settle into other people's lifestyles if they don't work for me.

I will not allow myself to be pressurized into what I don't want because the world or everyone around me is into that. *I am not everyone. I am not the whole world. I am me and it's very okay for me to be me.*

I have nothing to lose, but everything to gain in being me and embracing what works for me. I pledge to break all these limiting rules. I pledge to make my own relevant rules that work for me. This is my right and responsibility. I am responsible for how my life turns out.

In some cases, we do things the way everyone does them because we fear change. We can't stand the thought of change. *We always associate change with discomfort.* For this reason, we choose to settle for what we know: what we have always done; what other people are doing; what is being done around us.

We do things the way they are being done around

us because we fear how other people will look at us and what they will say when we do things differently from how they are being done. We want to please everyone at the expense of our lives.

You didn't come into this world to please everyone. People will look at you anyhow. People will always talk. They will talk when we do things right or in a wrong manner. People will have issues with what we do and with what we don't do. It's not easy to please or satisfy everyone. It's impossible.

Some people will never be pleased or satisfied regardless of what we do. Some people are hard to please or satisfy.

Some have decided not to be satisfied or pleased with anything we do. What can we do?

Do things in a way that works for you. You shouldn't do things because everyone does them that way. Doing things because of other people is neglecting ourselves and our welfare as individuals. This is one of the reasons the world has so many empty, miserable and unfulfilled people.

You can't achieve a true sense of purpose, meaning and fulfilment out of living someone's life.

It doesn't mean that everything that is being done by everyone or many people is the right thing. We can't say a certain method is perfect because many people use this method. It doesn't mean that we will all be successful because we use exhausted methods: we use methods that are being used by many people or everyone.

The rules or patterns we follow were made by human beings like us. We shouldn't just obey these rules or follow these patterns even when they don't work for us. We shouldn't observe these because everyone around us observes them: because those who came before us observed them.

We should understand who we are and what we want as individuals. We can't afford to obey these limiting rules. Dare to be a rule breaker. Dare to make your own rules that are relevant to you; that work for you.

5

SOMEONE MADE THESE RULES, SOMEONE MUST BREAK THEM

You can't spend a lifetime obeying every rule given to you by other people. The main reason for your creation and existence wasn't for you to obey these limiting rules. Some people came up with these rules and we don't know why they did.

Most of these limiting rules have been in existence for many generations. They have been observed faithfully in every generation. Some of these rules began when human beings came into existence.

After God made the first two people Adam and Eve, He told them how they should live. **Along the way, they felt that they couldn't live the way their Creator wanted them to live.** They disobeyed their Maker because they couldn't believe they could become or do what their Maker wanted them to become or do.

They thought through what their Maker had said to them. They saw things with a different point of view from how their Maker saw these things. This caused them to come up with their own rules. I don't know whether they knew that these were limiting rules. But they placed these limiting rules on themselves.

This laid a foundation for humanity to continue placing limiting rules on themselves. This made all human being who came after them to see these rules as a part of the human culture or tradition. These are some of the rules they came up with that caused them to disobey their Maker.

You can't become, do or achieve what your Maker wants. You are unable to become, do or achieve what He wants. You don't have what it takes to become, do or achieve what He wants. You are just human beings. You are only human. You are flesh and blood. You are unable to become, do or achieve what He wants because of your makeup.

They looked at themselves and concluded that they couldn't and were unable to live the way they should. As their descendants, we continue to observe the limiting rules they initiated as a part of the human culture or tradition.

Most of these limiting rules can be traced back to

our childhood. We learn about these rules from the time we start understanding things. A baby or child does or tries anything. They can enter any place.

They can touch the fire. They can eat or drink anything. They want to do anything and everything. They feel they can do anything and everything. They feel they can go to any place and do what they want.

When we are babies or little children we hear a lot of these. You can't do this or that. You shouldn't do this or that. You can't or shouldn't go here or there. You can't or shouldn't touch this or that. You can't or shouldn't eat this or that.

As children grow older, they take risks to do what they want. They see themselves as beings with the ability to do anything they want. Look at small children. They don't observe the limiting rules we observe. They have so much confidence in themselves; in their knowledge and abilities. They are fearless and courageous.

They see themselves as supermen, superheroes or magicians.

They believe they can jump on walls or anything.

They believe they can't use any stick as a magic stick to change anything into anything they want.

They believe they have everything it takes to become, do and achieve anything they want. They believe they know everything. **They even think they know better than their parents or older people.** They don't live to obey limiting rules.

When they become older enough we punish them for not obeying the limiting rules we place on them. They try to be superman or superhero and they fall terribly.

This is what they will hear or are likely to hear from older people. **Why did you do it? I told you not to do it. I told you that you couldn't do it. I told you that you are not able to do that.**

It's during these times and experiences that these children start seeing things the way we see them. They start believing that they can't become, do or achieve what they want. They believe they are unable to become, do or achieve what they want because they don't have what it takes.

They see a point in obeying every rule placed on them because they were made to believe that people always fail when they try to become, do or achieve what they want. They were only given limiting rules not encouraging or motivating rules.

These are the rules they were given every time they wanted to become, do or achieve something. You can't. You shouldn't. Don't. You are not able. You don't have. You don't know.

They were not given the rules that said, you can become, do or achieve what you want. You can become, do or achieve it. You are able to become, do or achieve it. You are the right person to become, do or achieve it. You have what it takes to become, do or achieve it.

They were only given negative, discouraging, limiting and destroying rules. They were not given positive, building, strengthening and encouraging rules.

Only one side of the coin was revealed to them. They were told one side of the story. Failure was more justified and exalted than success.

They were always made to see higher chances of failing than winning. They were only told the bad and the ugly part of falling. They were not told that it was also okay to fall, rise and try again. They were only taught that you fall and you quit.

They were only told that this falling was a sign that they couldn't climb: they were not the right person to climb; they didn't have what it took to climb; they were unable to climb; they shouldn't try to climb again.

In the process of all these, they accepted these limiting rules as a part of the human culture or tradition that should be observed by all human beings.

Most of these limiting rules are beliefs that we attach to the shortcomings that we link to our human makeup.

These limiting rules result from justifying, exalting and promoting what we are not, what we shouldn't be and what we can't be **over** who we are, who we should be and who we can be.

The rules result from justifying, exalting and promoting what we don't have, shouldn't have, can't have **over** what we have, should have and can have: what we don't do, didn't do, shouldn't do and can't do **over** what we do, can do and should do.

They result from justifying, exalting and promoting our inadequacies **over** our adequacies: our inabilities **over** our abilities; our weaknesses **over** our strengths; our failures **over** our success.

They result from justifying, exalting and promoting our challenges **over** our opportunities: our past experiences **over** our current experiences or what we can experience; the life we don't live, didn't live or have lived **over** the life we should live or can live.

- When we look at these, we can see that there are two options, but we always choose the negative **over** the positive.

- For most of us, it's easy to choose I can't become it **over** I can become it.
- I am not the right person **over** I am the right person.
- I don't have what it takes to do it **over** I have what it takes to do it.
- I can't do it **over** I can do it.
- I am not able **over** I am able.
- I am only human or flesh and blood **over** I am a spirit being or a god- the god of the earth.

We do this because we believe we have valid reasons that justify and support our decision to settle for limitations. We do this because this seems to be a part of the human culture or tradition that should be observed by everyone.

I believe there should be a balance in the rules we observe. We shouldn't only have rules that disadvantage, limit, discourage or destroy people. We should also have rules that can build, strengthen and encourage people. These should even be more than the disadvantaging rules.

As a rule breaker, I live in my world and realities. I exalt encouraging rules over discouraging rules. I may fail with these positive rules, but I don't easily settle for limiting rules. I don't live to promote these destroying rules.

In some cases, I can see that the situation I am dealing with is complex and that it won't be easy for me to do or achieve what I want. But I will still stick to believing that I can become, do or achieve what I want.

In some cases, I may fail to do what I believe I am able to do, but this doesn't bother me. I will be happy and proud of myself that I did the right thing.

These rules are terrible. They can encourage us to give up even before we try something. We look at the journey or the miles ahead and we give up before starting because we exalt these negative rules.

We look at the battle and we run away before we even try. **We have been made to believe that a battle means our defeat.** We were only told about the negative things that can happen in a battle. We were only told about the losses not the gains.

We haven't been told that we can also win a battle: that we can prepare for the battle and win it. We have been told from the beginning that we don't stand a chance in battles. We are not the right people, type or material to win this battle. We don't have what it takes to win this battle.

In some cases, we are told that we can't win or are unable to win because some people who were engaged in this kind of a battle didn't win. **It's unfortunate that we are always grouped into what**

we have nothing to do with. We need to understand that each of us is an individual; separate and independent.

We can't always be put in one box with everyone. We can't all be painted with one brush. Other people's failures shouldn't determine our outcome. So and so failed in what you are trying to do. You will also fail. Says who? This is unfair.

Each person should be given a chance: be allowed to try what they want to do. There is a sense of fulfilment that I get every time I try to do something. This is because I didn't give up looking at the situation. I tried. I gave myself a chance. I came out from this situation with valuable experiences and lessons I couldn't get otherwise.

In most cases, I don't even call this failure, but a learning ground where I gained valuable, knowledge, understanding, experience and wisdom.

These limiting rules are now a part of the human culture. They are a way of life for mankind. You look strange to other people when you break these rules. You face opposition and rejection when you defy these rules because you seem like a black sheep.

Everyone is going to the same direction but you are going to a different direction or you are going against them. Everyone sees things the same way and you see them differently.

Breaking the rules that existed for generations is like destroying the foundations that make you. It's like destroying the foundation of your life. It's like working against what makes you and the entire human race. When this is the case, you will face opposition and rejection from those who live to obey these rules.

People initiated these limiting rules. Some people initiated these rules after encountering certain challenges in what they wanted to do. Some came up with these rules after failing to become, do and achieve what they wanted.

People place these rules on everyone. They believe they should be observed by everyone. They believe they work for everyone. This is the reason many parents can't give their children a chance to be or do what they want.

Parents always use their failures to determine their children's outcome. They use their failures to discourage their children not to do what they want.

The problem with parents is that they don't see their children as individuals or separate independent human beings.

They see their children as their extensions that should live the way they lived or lived; do what they did the way they did it; start or continue where they ended; do and finish what they couldn't.

They look at all their failures and determine the kind of life and destiny their children should or shouldn't embrace. They use these to determine what their children should or shouldn't become, do or achieve during their lifetime.

You can't marry when you are twenty-one but thirty because I got married at thirty. You can't marry when you are forty when I got married at twenty-one. You can't dress that way because I have never dressed that way, even at your age. You can't do that business because you will fail. I tried it and failed. So, you also don't stand a chance.

The question is, will everyone in the world fail because you failed in a certain area? Who are you? Does it make sense to use your failure to determine other people's outcome?

Life should go on for others even when you have failed and are still failing. They have nothing to do with your failures. We shouldn't use our failures as rules and standards for everyone. Everyone has the right to determine the kind of life they want. We confuse our children and put them in trouble because of all these rules.

They will not achieve a true sense of purpose,

success, meaning and fulfilment in doing what we want them to do because that's not them. It's you living in or through them. You are making them to live your life.

It's unfair to deny your children the life and destiny they deserve. It's unfair to live your other life inside or through your children. It's unfair to make them live your life.

When will they live their lives when they are busy living yours. This lifetime is too short. No one should spend it living the life of another person.

In some cases, people came up with these limiting rules because of fear. They encountered fear in trying to become, do or achieve what they wanted. They came up with a rule that says you can't become it after they failed to become what they wanted to become.

They faced hardship in trying to become what they wanted to become. They ended up thinking that everyone will face these hardships in becoming who they want to be. They place these rules on you because they fear for you. They fear you will face the challenges and failures they faced.

They felt rejected by other people when they tried to become, do or achieve what they wanted. They give you these rules because they don't want you to go through rejection or encounter the challenges they encountered.

In some cases, they place these rules on you because this has become a way of life to them. They place these rules on you because they also had people who placed these rules on them. They do to you what was done to them.

They have been faithful in obeying these rules. They now believe that every person should obey all the rules placed on them. This is the reason people will have problems when you become different: when you do different things; when you do things differently.

They will have problems when you break rules in place. They will see you as someone who thinks he or she is better or smarter than other people. They will see you as someone who has a higher opinion of himself or herself.

They will think you are trying too hard to be something you are not. These are the reason they will place a rule that you can't become what you want to become.

I take my time to convert people or rule keepers into rule breakers because obeying these limiting rules hinders people from embracing their true identity, purpose, individuality and uniqueness.

Obeying these rules hinders people from becoming who they want to be or who they should be. Obeying these rules stops people from following their true purposes or dreams to follow those of other people.

You should be very careful. People will place bars above you and barriers before you and will tell you not to cross them. The life of a rule breaker is a life of defying and breaking limiting rules.

A rule breaker is a risk taker, barrier breaker, line crosser and record breaker. A rule breaker is a situation changer and a history maker.

Most of the rules placed on us are no longer relevant. They don't work for us. They don't work in our time and in the situations we encounter. We get inspiration based on our current situations.

We get inspiration to handle the situations we encounter. What is relevant to some people may not be relevant to some. What worked in a certain situation may not work in another situation.

The rules that worked for those who lived thousands of years ago may not work for us. Some no longer apply. We should break them and make our own rules that are relevant for us: that work for us.

DEALING WITH THE SPIRIT OF FOLLOWERSHIP

The journey to embracing your true self is not easy as it has enemies. The enemies will fight you up to a point where you will see a need to be like every other person around you. They will reduce you to be like everyone around you: be an ordinary person you never thought you could be; be a follower.

> *When the enemies of uniqueness are done with you, you will find yourself being counted among a group called "the rest".*

Do you know what "the rest" means? You are not counted among the important outstanding and exceptional people. What you do or achieve is not included among the outstanding or exceptional achievements.

You are a remainder, leftover or excess after the best people have been selected. Think of what happens to the leftover food after everyone has had enough. Excess means something that is not that important, significant, useful, valuable or needed after selecting the best things. Something you can easily do without.

Excess baggage is normally left behind after the most important things have been given a priority inside the main bag. People leave excess baggage at airports when they don't have enough money to pay for both the main and excess luggage.

The main reason for your creation and existence wasn't for you to spend a lifetime embracing the identity and purpose of an extra, alternative, reserve, spare part, substitute, standby, second hand, side thing, leftover, or backup plan.

You were not created and brought to this world just to be a follower, disciple, fan, deputy or assistant of everyone, every time and in everything.

You were created with the ability to do and achieve outstanding, exceptional or remarkable things. You are not even meant to be crying for other people to promote you. You are created to lead in your area or true purpose. You are the only one who can lead best in what you do.

Each of us has the seed of leadership and

greatness that should be discovered, nurtured and maximized.

You were made to lead with the help of the knowledge of your true identity and purpose. **No one was created to be a follower or to be led every time in everything.** You can be led or follow other people in areas that are not yours. You can be led by people of different identities and purposes.

There are leaders everywhere in our workplaces, places of worship, societies, clubs, or other organizations. This is all fine. No problem in following all these. **But you were also made to lead them in your true purpose, area or speciality.**

What is so wrong with you being followed by other people? Why should it always be you who should follow everyone around? Why should it be you who should always celebrate their great achievement and success?

It's perfectly okay to celebrate the success of other people. But is it wrong for you to be celebrated for your outstanding achievement in what you do? What makes you have faith, confidence, and trust in everyone's ability except yours?

Each of us has the seed of leadership and greatness. The main reason for your creation and existence is not for you to be a follower or disciple of anyone, anything, everyone, and everything in life and for life. You also have a life to live and lead.

> *You have a unique, special, and exclusive purpose that only you can fulfil and lead. You don't exist to increase followers in the world.*

The world has enough followers already and will do just fine with all these followers. **And we are on a mandate to turn these followers into leaders to reduce the number of followers in the world.**

Your true identity and purpose automatically make you a leader. These are leadership positions or offices. These give you the ability to lead in your own thing and way since you are different.

Sometimes, you don't need to be promoted into a certain position to be a leader. You don't always need to be in a higher or certain position for you to lead, be a leader, or be considered a leader. You don't always need promotion to lead.

Sometimes, you don't have to be called a leader for you to lead. You are a leader and you can lead even without a certain leadership position and title.

Being promoted to a certain higher position or being called a leader doesn't always make you a true, successful, great and fulfilled leader. You can be a great leader even without certain titles, positions or ranks. You can have power, control, and authority without badges.

Effective, successful and great leadership are not in positions, titles, badges, or promotion offer letters. These positions and titles are just platforms that help us unleash, maximize and fulfil the leader inside us.

Leadership is a spirit. These positions, titles and badges won't help us much when this leadership spirit is not there inside us or is not in good condition. You can't be an effective, successful leader without this spirit.

This is why it is believed that leadership is not for everyone. I believe what they mean is that you can't lead effectively without this spirit. The good news is that each of us can develop this spirit.

This leadership spirit is the inner leader that enables you to lead or be an effective, successful leader.

This spirit leads you to lead. The spirit will give you the conviction and confidence that you are a leader or can lead even with no one telling you this.

Ask the leaders you know. They will tell you they became leaders because they had the conviction that they were leaders and could lead. This leadership spirit reveals to you the seed of leadership within you that you need to discover, nurture and maximize for you to become an effective successful leader.

The success of your leadership depends on the condition of this leadership spirit. It's your responsibility to ensure that you develop this spirit for it to help you become the successful leader you can be, should be or are meant to be.

Of course, certain positions give you more and better opportunities to lead than those who are not in these positions. You can lead in anything you do, even when you are under someone.

This is not to make anyone feel bad, but reveal what enemies of different thinking and progress can do to ignorant people. This happens when forces against your uniqueness and greatness fight and defeat you. Maybe you have heard this before?

He was very passionate, active, strong, and motivated when he joined this company, but now he is just like every other person in the company? Didn't we say he should take things easy like everyone else here?

Didn't we say this is just being a newly employed excited youth in a new company? Didn't we say he will come back or down to where everyone else is? Didn't we tell him that what he was doing was common for everyone who found a new job?

We told him that this excitement will wear off with time. Now he has forgotten about those brilliant ideas he had for this company. Now he is like all of us here. We knew he would end up joining the crowd, anyway.

We told him to take things easy and relax like all of us. He thought he was smarter. He wanted to get the attention and favour of the management team. Didn't we tell him this is real life?

He was very active when he joined this church. I don't know what is happening to him these days. He never used to miss even one church service, but this thing called life has reduced him to being a Sunday churchgoer.

He used to spit fire every time he preached, but these days he preaches like other preachers in town. He used to perform an unusual miracle every time he ministered to people. Sicknesses couldn't stand his presence. Now we don't know what happened. He is like any other preacher.

His business used to be more successful than any business in this area, but now it's like all the other businesses around. He used to provide exceptional customer service, but these days he runs his restaurant like all the other restaurants around.

He was named the best musician for three years in a row. But drugs have reduced him to be like any other person in the rehabilitation centre. He doesn't even have anything because he sold everything he had for drugs.

Their marriage used to be so successful, but now it's like any other marriage around. He was the best in school, but now he is just like any other student. There are higher chances of encountering challenges or forces that are against you becoming the unique person you want to be, should be, or are meant to be.

These are enemies of your true identity, purpose and uniqueness. When you embrace your true identity and purpose, you will differ from other people. This is because true identity and purpose are revealed to your inner person or discovered from within.

You are the only one who has access to your inner person. **The life you live should display the unique person you discovered from inside you.** This is meant to make each of us unique or different. This is meant to diversify humanity, balance and complete the world, to make it the best place it can be for all of us.

The major problem we face is people who don't even try to discover this inner person or give him a chance to do his assignment in our lives. What they want is to copy and imitate other people.

Many people are into this business of copying and pasting other people onto themselves. This is where you wait for other people to discover their true identity and purpose, and you copy and paste these discoveries onto yourself. You wait for other people to become themselves for you to become them. A miserable business indeed!

You are on a mission to become whatever is being discovered by other people. It doesn't matter what that is. This is the reason someone can be pulled into crime easily.

Someone decided that being a criminal is their identity, and crime is their purpose, and the next thing you do is join them. You copy and paste their thing onto yourself. This is identity and purpose crises. You may go through identity and purpose crises because of ignorance.

The good news is that everyone can discover their true identity and purpose if they want to. There is that mine deep inside you, where you can discover great and valuable discoveries that can change your life for better forever.

Things may look difficult, but they are possible. The difficulty of something doesn't determine its impossibility. There is hope for everyone. You are not destined for the identity of a follower.

Following is not your true purpose for life. Reject the follower mentality and embrace your uniqueness. **The followership spirit will tell you that you are meant to be a follower, not a leader.** For this reason, you can't be a unique person; do or achieve anything unique.

You should live to follow others: become what everyone around you is becoming; do what everyone is doing. This followership spirit is an enemy of your uniqueness. You need to be able to identify it in your life for you to deal with it effectively.

7

DEALING WITH THE FEAR TO BE DIFFERENT

The Fear To Be Different

The fear of being unique or different from other people is one of the great enemies of our uniqueness. This fear causes many people not to become the unique or different people they should be or are meant to be.

Some people are not aware of this kind of fear. Some live in denial of it. Some know very well that it exists and that it haunts them. Some think it's normal and okay to have this kind of fear.

Some believe it's a part of life. Some believe you can't overcome this fear. Some are slaves to this fear. There is nothing they do without asking themselves what people will think or say.

- This fear of differing from other people refers to the fear of becoming who you know you should be because of other people.
- You don't become yourself because you fear to differ from other people.
- You fear the challenges that come along with being different.
- You know the kind of an identity you want to embrace, but you have fear because if you become who you want to be, you will differ from those around you.
- You don't want to appear strange to other people.
- You fear the possibility of lack of acceptance, approval and support.
- You fear the possibility of being rejected every time you think of embracing your true identity or uniqueness.

If you embrace your true identity, you will automatically differ from other people. You won't fight or struggle to be unique. This will come easy as it's a part of you. People will notice that you differ from others.

You get the knowledge of your true identity from inside you. You know you are meant to be different, but you find yourself being like other people in everything. This is because it's like it's a part of us to adapt to and be influenced by things around us.

From the time a baby or child is old enough to notice things around him that is when influencing and adapting begin. They are influenced by anything, anyone, or everything around them.

They adapt to anyone and everyone around them. They start from their family members, their friends throughout schooling, and up to just anyone they meet in the journey of life.

They adapt to people they know, strangers, media people, or just anyone who leaves an impression on them. These continue in the workplace, church, societies, or clubs.

These things that started from babyhood continue as a habit, and it reaches a point where it's believed to be a part of life.

If you hear someone stressing the need to be unique, you just don't understand what they are trying to say. You just don't get it when you are advised and encouraged to discover and embrace your uniqueness.

You don't understand people should be that different from each other. You don't know this is how things should be. You think people are the same just that some choose to be different or do different things.

You don't see the possibility of each member of the human race having his true identity, purpose or destiny. You don't see the possibility of each person being unique or different from other people.

What makes each of the over seven billion people to look different physically can make them different inside them.

What makes each of us have unique fingerprints can make each of us unique and different from other people.

The physical difference is a sign that each of us differs from each other. Each person has the same body parts as everyone, but we look different from each other. These differences say it all about us being made different people.

You don't see uniqueness as something that can be achieved because you have been in the business of copying and adapting since babyhood. This is like a part of you now.

Being encouraged to be unique is like a new philosophy to you. It's like a foreign idea. It feels like you are being asked to crumble the structures you have built for many years.

You don't see yourself as a unique, separate, and

independent person. It's difficult for you to personalize, singularize, and individualize yourself. You can't distinguish yourself from the crowd.

The copying and adapting habit have created a crowd mentality in you. You can't be decisive or resolute without the input of other people. You need the input and approval of other people for you to become a particular person or do a particular thing.

The fear of differing from other people is right inside you. You are not embracing your uniqueness because you are the one fighting yourself from becoming the unique person you are meant to be.

If this fear is too strong in you, it will be very difficult for you to become yourself. You are your enemy in this case. Unfortunately, this inner enemy is with you twenty-four hours daily.

It takes a lot to fight enemies that are inside you than external enemies.

It takes a lot to fight inner enemies than it takes to fight enemies in the form of other people.

If its other people preventing you from becoming who you want to be, you can choose to stay away from them until your true identity is well established and settled within you. **But how do you stay away from yourself?** This is where making firm, clear cut choices and decisions come in.

People don't become who they want to be or should be because they fear other people. The thought of what they will think or say if you become who you want to be steals the little good things you have inside you.

You fear what they will do to you: what they will think about you; how they will look at you; how you will appear to them; what they will say in you becoming the person you want to be, should be, or are meant to be.

And the question is, so what if they talk? Is it your business if they think and look at you the way they choose to? What is wrong with everyone doing what they know best?

This is what you should do. Work very hard on becoming the best you can be, while they think and talk about you the best they can. We will see who will benefit positively.

And how do you know that these people are talking or will talk about you if you become yourself or the unique person you should be? Be sure you are not a culprit in this regard.

If you talk more about other people negatively, you will always believe the same thing is being done to you.

You have the experience in this kind of

business. You know how this brutal business works.

If you know you are innocent of this business or you are doing the right thing, you won't care about people talking about you. If they choose to do it, fine. It's none of your business. This doesn't stop you from being who you want to be and living your life abundantly.

It's normal or common to think that other people are looking at you in a certain way. You think this way even when they are not doing it. This means you can put your life to a standstill because you believe some people are talking about you.

You limit your progress because you believe there is a certain way some people look at you. In this case, you are concerned, worried, troubled, and stressed about what you shouldn't.

> You consider those who never consider you when they live their lives and do their things. You waste your precious time and strength on people who don't spend theirs on you when they live their lives. You hold yourself captive because of those who never hold themselves captive because of you.

You are not being fair to yourself. You are your enemy. You have a very serious problem if you fear what they will think about you if you become this or do that.

The problem is, you have no access to their thinking faculty. You can't control how everyone thinks. People have the ability and freedom to think about anything, everything, anyone, everyone, including you.

Maybe they have this right. They can do this anyhow, anytime, and as often as they want. There is nothing anyone, *including you,* can do about this, except to learn to live with this.

If you put your life on hold because you are concerned about how people look at you then you have a serious problem. The question is, how do you want them to look at you? What if that is their innocent way of looking at people? Will you stop living your life because of their way of looking?

I was a frequent customer in a certain business place. An argument that led to a serious quarrel broke up because the business owner didn't approve how the customer looked at her. The argument was so serious that the customer threatened the business owner about going to report the poor customer service to the consumer affairs department or police.

I could see the shock on the face of the customer. The quarrel continued up to a point where all customers stopped, all they were doing to watch and listen. One employee intervened. To cut the story short, the business owner ended up apologizing because the situation could put the business in a very bad position.

You can't affect what your life depends on because of how other people look at you. People will look at you anyhow they want, and there is nothing you or anyone can do about it.

It's not good to have this fear because you have no control over these people and their way of looking. Why can't you live your life the way you want and they continue to look at you the way they want?

I still insist that sometimes what we see is not it. It's possible to conclude that people are looking at you in a certain way when they are not giving you that kind of look. This may be what is engraved inside you.

Maybe one person or a few people gave you that look in the past. Maybe this past look made you very uncomfortable up to a point where you hate it so much. What looks like it makes you very uncomfortable.

Even when you don't understand the look given to you by other people, you conclude it's that kind of look that you hate so much. All the looks you don't understand or approve, you push them into the category of the looks you abhor.

It's possible to see, sense, or pick up a problem

where there is no problem at all because you have inner unresolved issues. **Other people become scapegoats because of these inner issues.**

People with inner unresolved issues are a challenge. **You step on them by mistake, and hell breaks loose, fire comes out and explodes.** You try to apologize and instead of them accepting your apology and moving on, they will quarrel until everyone is aware of this quarrel.

Some are so good at quarrelling, so much that everyone and the world around them will stop to listen to them. You listen to the cause of the quarrel and you are like, there is no issue here. *These are people with unresolved issues- anger and bitterness.*

You touch what concerns them you have pressed a wrong button. They boil and explode over minor issues. This is just to stress the point I talked about above. This is how I conclude what we just discussed.

Take stock of your life. Put your inner house in order because the problem may not be with other people but you. Let people talk. Let them think about what they want to think about. Let them look at you the way they want. Their look will take nothing from you. I seriously don't see this as a problem.

Are you the only one in the world who is being talked about or looked at? Are you not looking at other people? You haven't talked about anyone at all?

What does their thinking, looking, or talking has to do with you? How is it your business? How does it stop you from becoming yourself and fulfilling your purpose? How does it prevent you from achieving a sense of fulfilment out of life?

The journey of a different thinker or a rule breaker is not an easy one. It's not easy to change some things that make us or the foundations we are built on. We don't choose what we are born into. This includes family and situations. We don't choose the way they raise us.

But when we grow and mature, we can choose what we want in or out of life. We can choose how we want to live our lives. But this is not easy. This is what different thinkers and rule breakers have to face to become and do what they want.

This is what I experienced as a different thinker and a rule breaker. You face fierce battles for choosing to rebel against your foundations. This battle is not for the fainthearted.

- It needs someone who can be resolute; who can make clear cut firm choices and decisions concerning what they want and how they want to live.
- It needs people who will not be discouraged

easily.

- People who can refuse to bow or give up regardless of the challenges involved.
- People who can refuse to go away even when challenges are at their peak.
- Those who will not be put out, down, and off easily by circumstances.
- People who have resolved to be unshakable and unstoppable in becoming who they want to be or living the lives they want.
- It needs those with the strength of mind and character.
- Those who can dig their heels deeper enough into the ground to stand for what they believe in.
- It needs those who will not be contained and limited by the circumstances of this life.
- You need to be emotionally strong to stand for what you believe in.
- You need to have the audacity to stand for what you want.
- You need to have some nerve, spine, or brass neck to make it in this life. It's not easy.

The Fear To Do Different Things

Many people fear doing things that differ from those done by other people around them. The adapting mentality we grew up with from babyhood wants us to do only what everyone is doing around us.

How to Identify this Fear

- We are only comfortable when we do things that are the same or similar to what other people are doing.
- We don't feel good when we do what we feel led to do from inside us.
- We don't feel comfortable when we change what has always been done in a certain way.
- We are uncomfortable when what we do stands out from the rest of the things that are being done around us.
- We don't feel good when what we do looks like it's not related, linked, or connected to what every other person is doing around us.
- We feel uncomfortable when what we do looks or seem incomparable, inimitable, matchless, unique, rare, or the only one of its kind among those we associate with.
- We are comfortable when we do and achieve the same things that we have always achieved or what everyone is doing and achieving.

- We are comfortable with the normal, common, and usual things that are also done in a normal, common, and usual way.
- We only accept things that are identical, equal, matching, and undistinguishable.
- Whatever we want to do, we will always try to match it up with what is in place.
- The things we do should be impossible to differentiate from what is available or is being done by everyone.
- We prefer things to be left the way they are or in their original state.
- We believe it is okay for everyone to copy or imitate anything, anyone, everyone, and everything.
- We always pursue the same philosophy that has been used or is being used around us.
- We follow the same exhausted pattern, approach and way of doing things.
- We will still use the same method, even if those who used or use it have failed and keep failing.
- We will still use the same principles and standards even when they don't work for us, but because everyone is using them.

What is wrong with introducing different practices

and traditions that we want or will yield the best results? Is there anything wrong in following your different ideas, desires, dreams, and ways of doing things?

Where is the problem in understanding things your way up to a point where you do them your way? There is nothing wrong with having your exclusive opinions, assessments, judgements, and conclusions on matters.

It's okay to have your own set of rules in what you want to do because the rules you found in place have been set by someone else. If they work best for you go for them.

You can operate and succeed with a different set of rules that you set for yourself. You can have your exclusive, independent, personalized, and individualized thoughts, philosophies and strategies.

People may or will initially have a problem with you doing different things, but will get used to you and what you do with time. They will see the importance of what you do and the way you do it, up to a point where they will love and support it.

People will recognize and respect you for being unique: having something to stand up for; standing out from the rest of the people; daring to be unique or having the audacity to be different.

Most of us desperately want to please just anyone and everyone, even when we don't need or have to. We compromise the most important things that our lives depend on because we are dying to please just anyone and everyone. We lose where we could gain because of the thought of what other people will think or say about us.

There is this common saying every time someone wants to do something different. Yes, we hear what you are trying to say and we understand the changes you want to bring into this organization. But this is how we do things here. And they should be kept this way. This is our vision and it should be followed the way everyone has been following it for many years.

Have you forgotten that this is how we do things in this family? This is how we run our family. We don't want anything different. This is how we cook and eat in this family. And it's the same recipe they have used since the family started. They are not ready to eat anything different, nicer, or healthier.

This is how I raise my children and no one has anything to say in how I raise them. And you are like; no wonder this family is dysfunctional. Have you forgotten how our great grandparents ran this family company since its inception? And they don't even consider if this may be the reason this business hasn't been growing for many years.

We will run this country this way because it has always been run this way. We don't want any different idea because the ones we have always had in place serves us just fine. People are very comfortable with things that have been done, used, and repeated over and over again.

We prefer things that have been exhausted: that no longer need much creativity and effort; where not much is being experienced and learnt in the process of what we do.

We don't want to sweat, so we just copy and paste what is readily available. We don't care about great things that may come with doing different things or doing things differently.

We are into following crowds and maintaining their patterns and routines. All we want is to maintain what has always been done for us to fit in. We fear doing a different thing or doing things differently because we don't know what will happen when we do this. We are sure of what has always been done because it can maintain what we have.

The spirit of managing and maintaining the same things is the enemy of progress.

This is an enemy of our uniqueness. You maintain and manage what is in place. There is no place for different, new or better things. There is no place for improvement, development, and growth in maintaining the same things and the same ways of doing them.

In other words, this is what people are indirectly saying. **We want to keep the limitations we have been having.** We would rather be disadvantaged by these limitations than do different things or do things differently.

We expect everyone to fry every fish and potato. The one who uses the roasting method or other methods of cooking will be looked at in a certain way. This is because everyone is used to the frying method. The roasted food won't be fully accepted, even if they may be tastier or healthier.

It's common for us to reject the things we are not used to or those we don't understand. People want or expect all members of the human race to use the same path throughout our lifetime. We are expected to take the same route our family or community members have always taken.

People will fear for you if you pave your path or use a different route from the one used by everyone.

They fail to understand why you invite problems into your life by doing what hasn't been done or doing things differently.

I know what I am talking about here. This book

results from what I learnt and experienced over the years. It seems like people never understood what I wanted from the time I completed high school.

As a result, I faced immense disapproval, opposition, and different kinds of challenges. Some people were against me becoming myself or differing from other people.

It's normal for us to disapprove, oppose, criticize, and reject what we don't understand. Problems intensify when what they don't understand seems different.

I am one of those people who were told to sit down like any other person: to be like other people, otherwise, I was inviting more trouble to myself; to relax and enjoy myself like any other youth of my age. You know where you are told to become and do things like other people's children? I was told to take things easy for the reasons they had.

I was told that I may be the only one taking things too seriously or the way I took them. They gave me the examples of people who were taking things easy.

It's like people had in mind what I should become or do in life. It was difficult for some people to accept that I may have a different identity and purpose from those they wanted for me. Maybe they didn't see me as an individual or a person who also had the right to choose and a life to live.

Maybe they didn't understand there was a thing called true identity, purpose or destiny. They didn't understand that each of us is different and that they should accept things that way. Maybe they thought I was everyone or like everyone. They expected me to embrace identities that weren't mine. These were identities I knew nothing about. These were things I couldn't possibly become.

What they wanted me to become and do would make me feel like an imprisoned slave. *I would feel like I had no life.* I had no provision, strength, and ability to become or do what they wanted. I had no resources reserved for the destiny they wanted me to embrace.

They couldn't understand I had a different identity and purpose that I needed to embrace. **Something difficult for me to run away from as it was within me. Something too strong for me to ignore.** Of course, I tried many times to run away from this at the beginning.

The first person to reject that kind of route was me. I rejected my true identity and purpose immediately I discovered it. I believe some disapproved my path because of a lack of knowledge and understanding.

I also rejected it at the beginning because of the lack of sufficient understanding. You know where you discover that you need to go somewhere and you immediately reject the journey without enough information? This is what I did. Even after having enough information concerning my destiny, I still had issues because other people had issues with it.

I was told that so and so tried and that I should look at where they were. I was told they failed in trying to do things that were not being done in their families or communities.

You know where you are told this thing will wear off with time because you are just being a youth. I was told that the people who were into what I wanted or something similar didn't take things the way I did. They took things easy.

I was told that there will still be some other people who will do what I wanted to do, even if I didn't do it. My doing it wouldn't make that much difference in the world.

Others thought because it looked like I was into something different, I had a higher opinion of myself. They made me feel as if I thought I was better or smarter than other people: higher than the highest; the creator of this thing I wanted to do; the beginning and end of this thing.

What I know And Say About Myself

What was said to me or about me shook my core. These made me very uncomfortable because I was young, weak, and immature. Now that I am grown up and mature, I just don't care. I don't care what anyone thinks about me and what I do.

I know who I am. I understand my true identity and purpose as an individual. This is so established, grounded, and settled inside me. It's engraved inside me. No one has access or the ability to touch or erase it. I am very confident about my true identity, purpose and destiny. I am so in love with these.

My destiny is the perfect thing my Creator did for me; the greatest honour our Creator can give to a human being.

I am satisfied. I don't wish for something different from my true identity, purpose and destiny.

Now I can fearlessly, confidently, unapologetically, unashamedly and proudly say this. **Yes, I am the beginning and end of my true identity, purpose and destiny. I am the first and last in this thing.**

People may look like me and do something similar to what I do. They may have some things in common with me. They may put me in the same category with other people but I can say these fearlessly, confidently, unapologetically, unashamedly and proudly.

- Yes, I am the only me.
- I am the only one of my kind.
- The only original authentic version of myself.
- I come once in a lifetime.
- There will never be another me or someone exactly like me in this generation or the next generations.
- There has been no one exactly like me in the past.
- What I have is exclusive to me.
- I am a particular person, and there is something particular about me.
- I am a very important person; a VVIP.
- I am a unique and rare kind; a very mysterious mystery.
- I exist as a supply to a particular demand that compelled my creation and existence.
- I am here on a divine arrangement, appointment and assignment.
- I am not a slip into this world.
- I am perfectly scheduled.
- This generation desperately needs me. It

couldn't and can't do without me.

- The next generations can't do without me. This is the reason I have been sent before them to put some things in place for them before they come. My Creator trusts me to lay a proper foundation for them.
- I am very special. I am not a nobody.
- I have a true identity to embrace and a true demanding purpose to fulfil.

Nothing and no one, including you, can do anything about the above. The knowledge I have about myself makes me not to take myself lightly. It makes me a different thinker and a rule breaker.

It gives me the ability to distinguish myself from other people. It gives me the ability to singularize, personalize or individualize myself. This makes me have a higher opinion of myself.

The complete knowledge of myself is limited to me. I know and understand what no one does about me. For this reason, I will continue to give myself the best respect, treatment and honour that I deserve or is fit for a person like me. I will talk good about myself because there are best things I know about myself.

I can't fully expect these from other people. They can't fully honour what they don't understand. This is the reason what other people do or say about me doesn't move me an inch. What they say doesn't make any difference in me. **I am so full of myself.** All these in a good way, though.

Now, what I just said about myself is not really about me. This book is not all about me. I wrote it for you. It's about you. So, I encourage you to understand and see yourself the way I talked about myself.

Replace my I with your I in everything I said about myself. This is how you are meant to understand and see yourself. You are a very important, unique and special person.

You shouldn't fear to be different or do the different things you want because of other people. The people you fear or regard so much have nothing to offer you. They can't give you a true sense of purpose, meaning and fulfilment out of life.

These may be those who don't even consider you when they live their lives or do what they want. Why should you? These are enemies of your uniqueness that you should identify and deal with.

Discover, understand, embrace and maximize your uniqueness. Live your life your way. Do your things your way. This is your life. This is the only life and lifetime that you have. You need to maximize it and get the most out of it.

Don't allow the fear of other people to stop you from doing the different things you want to do, should do, or are meant to do.

Your genuine sense of purpose, meaning and fulfilment out of life depends on this. You don't owe anyone an explanation or apology of how you live your life, what you choose to do, and how you choose to do it.

You have nothing to apologize about. You are not an apologist. You don't exist to apologize for who you become and how you live your life.

Embrace your true self- individuality, identity, purpose and uniqueness confidently, courageously, unapologetically, unashamedly and proudly.

This is your only chance. You have one life and lifetime.

THEY BECAME SUCCESSFUL BECAUSE THEY BROKE RULES

Everyone has been given some limiting rules. Different people deal with these rules differently. Most people don't realize that these are limiting rules. They see these as a part of life.

Most people don't question these rules. They live to obey every rule even if it disadvantages. But there are those who have pledged to defy, bend and break these limiting rules. And they go on to make their own rules that work for them.

Different people are where they are in their lives depending on how they deal with these limiting rules. What we become, do or achieve is determined by how we deal with these rules. Our outcome- failure or success is determined by how we deal with these limiting rules.

These rules are at a point where they are seen as a part of the human belief, culture or tradition. This is a serious problem because we have been made to believe that culture or tradition is something that should be respected and observed by everyone. **Culture is a very powerful force.** Most of the things we do are mainly influenced by culture.

There are some people who have looked through these limiting rules and decided to do something about them. They vowed to defy, disobey, reject and rebel against these rules. They vowed to break these limiting rules to become, do or achieve what they should. They vowed to become rule breakers.

I have made a vow to be a rule breaker and to live as one. I have also made a vow to raise a generation of rule breakers.

I am on a mission to raise a rare breed of individuals who will defy all odds to become who they believe they should be: to do what they believe they should do; to achieve what they believe they should achieve; to live the life they believe should live.

I am on a mission to raise rule breakers in a form of barrier breakers, line crossers and record breakers: to raise pacesetters, recorder makers and breakers; to raise situation changers, world changers, history changers and makers.

These are rule breakers because they have to defeat challenges in place to become, do or achieve what they want.

To become a rule breaker you need to be a different thinker. You need to be able to see things differently for you to become a different thinker. You need to be able to look at things, see and understand them differently.

You need to be able to look at things from a different angle and see them from a different perspective. You need to be able to differentiate opposites: a disadvantage from an advantage.

Each of us has been given some limiting rules. What differentiates us is how we deal with these rules.

One thing is clear. The people who obey rules and those who break rules differ from each other. They look at things differently. They see and understand things differently. They think differently. They live in different worlds and realities. This is the reason they don't easily understand and accept each other.

Some people who live in our time have pledged to break these limiting rules for them to become, do or achieve what they want. Some people who lived in the past broke the limiting rules that everyone lived by. They became, did and achieved what they wanted because they broke these rules.

They are called history changers and makers because they did what most people didn't do. They defeated the pressure to be like everyone around them who obeyed rules.

They made history by breaking the rules that were observed by everyone as a part of the human culture and tradition. They made history by broking the rules that existed for many centuries. They broke the rules that disadvantaged people around them.

Think of all the people who are considered as great achievers or history makers. They are all known for a particular thing. They are known to have defied all odds to become, do or achieve what they wanted.

Think of the great achievers, creators, inventors and innovators you know or have read about. They defied odds to do and achieve these. They withstood opposition and rejection to become, do and achieve what they wanted.

The ability to become, do and achieve what they wanted amid opposition, disapproval, and discomfort made them great people. Think of all the great achievements we have that make our lives better and comfortable.

The first person to try to invent a flying machine or an aircraft didn't have things easy. I believe people gave him many rules that could discourage him.

You want to invent a flying machine? For what? Why do you want to do that? Where have you seen a flying machine? Why should you do what hasn't been done before?

You can't do it. You are unable to do it. You shouldn't do it. Forget about flying machines and do what everyone around us is doing. I don't think you will be successful because no one has ever done that.

I just don't see it going up. I don't see it flying. I see it crushing before you know it. Why should you place yourself out there for disappointment, frustration and embarrassment? **I wouldn't try that if I were you.**

This person obviously broke all the limiting rules placed on him by people or logic to do and achieve what he wanted. He became successful in what he wanted to do and achieve because he was a rule breaker.

Think of all the trains, vehicles and other modes of transport. Think of all the magnificent breathtaking buildings we have around the world. Think of the means of communication we have today. Some people initiated and invented all these. These people didn't have things easy.

Some were reminded about their ages when they revealed what they wanted to become, do or achieve. Some were told that they were too young for what they wanted to become, do or achieve. They were told to take things easy and relax like their age mates.

Others were told that they were too old to become, do or achieve want they wanted. They were reminded that they had no strength to do what they wanted to do. Rule breakers don't regard this kind of rules.

I have seen genius children who achieved great success in what they did. They became famous at a very young age. I have seen great child actors, actresses and singers. There are children authors.

Imagine telling Michael Jackson at the age of five that he didn't stand a chance to be successful in music because he was too young to sing. Imagine placing the "you can't rule" on him.

Imagine telling him to relax and delay his passion for singing like other kids of his age in the neighbourhood or community. Imagine telling him that he didn't have what it took to be a successful musician.

He became extremely successful. Imagine if he obeyed all the limiting rules that people placed on him because of his age.

I have seen people who were involved in races at the age of seventy. There were people who were not happy with this. They wondered why these old people couldn't retire, relax and take things easy like their age mates. They didn't understand why these old people did this. They didn't know that these people gained a sense of purpose, meaning and fulfilment from these races.

Look at the Paralympic champions we have today. Think about those without legs. I am reminded of Oscar Pistorious, *the blade runner* from South Africa. Do you think everyone agreed with them when they revealed their desire to take part in sports?

People had questions for them. **But the legs?** Why would you do that? How are you going to do it? You can't do it. You are not able to run. You don't have what it takes. You are not the right person. You don't have legs. Forget about this and look for a job where you can sit on and do your work.

They are being celebrated today because they broke the limiting rules that logic and other people placed on them looking at their physical condition.

They can run faster than most people with legs. They became a success story because they broke all the limiting rules they were given. People should be given a chance to become, do or achieve what they want.

The Holy Bible is the final authority and standard for my life because it contains the mind of my Creator concerning me.

It reveals my true identity: who I am, who I should be; who I am meant to be; who I can be; who I will become. I am what it says I am. I can be what it says I can be. I will be what it says I should be; I will be what it says I will be. I am the right person to become this. I have what it takes to become this.

It reveals what I have: what I should have; what I am meant to have; what I can have; what I will have. I have what it says I have: I can have what it says I can have. I will have what it says I should have; I will have what it says I will have. I am the right person to have this. I have what it takes to have this.

It reveals what I should do: what I am meant to do; what I can do; what I will do. I do what it says I should do: I can do what it says I can do; I am able to do and will do what it says I should do; I will do what it says I will do. I am the right person to do this. I have what it takes to do this.

It reveals what I should achieve: what I am meant to achieve; what I can achieve; what I will achieve. I achieve what it says I should achieve: I can achieve what it says I can achieve; I will achieve what it says I will achieve. I am the right person to achieve this kind of achievement. I have what it takes to achieve this.

It reveals the life I should live: the life I am meant to live; the life I can live; the life I will live. I live the life it says I should live: I can live the life it says I can live; I will live the life it says I will live. I am the right person to live this kind of life. I have what it says to live this life.

The matter is settled if my Maker doesn't place limiting rules on me. I won't allow anyone to place limiting rules on me because they didn't make me. They don't understand what I have inside me.

They don't understand me: what I can become; what I can do; what I can achieve. If the Bible doesn't say someone can't do music at the age of five or hundred then it can be done. The matter is settled.

People will not approve or support what you want to become, do or achieve, but your pledge to be a rule breaker will help you through. People gave limiting rules to great achievers and history makers when they started their journeys to greatness.

Imagine if they didn't break these rules. Imagine if they didn't make their own rules. They achieved great success because they broke rules to become, do or achieve what they wanted.

Think about the late former president of South Africa, Mr Nelson Mandela. I imagine the first time he revealed his dream to become the president of South Africa. I believe people told him different stories that could discourage him. They placed limiting rules on him. Some told him this was an impossible mission looking at the situation that time.

This man decided to break the rules to become, do and achieve what he wanted. He stayed for many years in prison because of his desire for change. But this didn't cause him to agree with their opinion that he didn't stand a chance in what he wanted.

I believe he understood who he was. He understood his Creator. He didn't see anywhere in the Bible where it said a black person shouldn't become, couldn't become and wasn't able to become the president of South Africa in those situations during those times.

Some people thought he was out of his mind and that is why they put him in prison for that long. Many people had died trying to get the freedom that this man wanted. These fallen heroes are still celebrated in South Africa for their bravery.

This man achieved his dream because he pledged to defy and break limiting rules placed on him by other people, realities, circumstances and logic.

Some people made a rule that said there won't be a black president, and this is why they made things difficult for him to become one. But he made a rule that said there will be a black president, and that he will be this president. Imagine if he didn't break the rules. Imagine if he didn't make his own rules.

Think about the former US president Barack Obama. I believe he faced similar challenges faced by Mr Mandela. I believe many people couldn't believe it when he first revealed his intention to become the first African American president.

They didn't see that happening. They saw this as an impossible mission. They wondered why he couldn't relax and enjoy his senator position and forget about the presidency thing.

This man suffered great opposition. He was even told that he wasn't a true American. They were convinced that he didn't stand a chance. They saw this as a waste of time and other resources.

But this nearly impossible dream was fulfilled because he was faithful to the pledge he made to be a rule breaker and to live as one. Being a rule breaker made him a history maker. Imagine if this man obeyed the limiting rules that were placed on all African Americans.

The journey to making this history wasn't a smooth one, but he stayed true to what he believed and wanted not what other people believed and wanted. He gave a chance to the rules he made for himself not those placed on him by other people.

When we look at it, this man fulfilled one rule breaker's dream. Martin Luther King. This man had a dream for African Americans to have freedom like other Americans.

> He died for breaking the rule that said African Americans didn't deserve the freedom, equality, success and greatness enjoyed by white people.
>
> He was killed by those who were uncomfortable with him defying the belief that black people were inferior to white people.
>
> He was killed for his dream and for the power and influence that this dream had.

Imagine if Mr King didn't break the rules that were placed on the African American community. Things are not as disconnected from each other as we think. Barack Obama managed to become the first black president because a rule breaker came up with a dream that defied rules against black people.

Mr King didn't live to see the fulfilment of his dream, but he had faith that it would be achieved even after he had passed on. This is because he had given birth to other rule breakers who continued with his dream in his absence. This is the power of rule breaking.

He had raised a generation of rule breakers who had pledged not to allow other human beings to place limiting rules on them because of the colour of their skin.

This reminds me of Mahatma Gandhi of India. This man fought tirelessly and went through a lot of challenges for India to gain its independence from the British rule. There was a rule that said Indians were going to continue being a British colony.

This man broke this rule and made his own rule that said India should and will be independent. He went through a lot of challenges to achieve his dream. **He died while breaking the British rule. He died while fulfilling the rule he initiated.** He didn't live to enjoy the results of his labour but his mission was accomplished.

Things are not always easy for rule breakers. Imagine if these people didn't break the limiting rules placed on them. Take a minute and think about this. Looking at the people we talked about, it's clear that what they wanted was close to impossible.

What they did was like fighting the foundation that made them. The African Americans we talked about fought against the US: its foundations, beliefs, culture, traditions, practices, laws, systems and the government. This is not easy. In this book, we will not hide behind a finger.

Embracing the life of a rule breaker is not easy. This is like one person fighting against foundations, setups, systems, mindsets, beliefs, cultures, traditions or governments.

Many people didn't really understand me. Some people concluded that I had a problem though they didn't understand this problem. I never admitted to them that I had a problem, but I seriously had a problem. **My major problem was that I was a different thinker and rule breaker.**

I had pledged to break all the rules that hindered me from becoming who I wanted to be: who I believed I should be or was meant to be. I had pledged to break all the rules that hindered me from doing and achieving what I wanted: what I believed I should do and achieve or was meant to do and achieve.

My problem was that I couldn't obey and I wasn't able to obey the rules that other people around me obeyed. I had the right to do this. Everyone has a reason for doing what they do. People have their reasons for obeying limiting rules. They have the right to choose to obey or break these rules.

I also have reasons for breaking the rules that don't work for me and for making the rules that work for me. I have this right to choose. I went against all odds to do what I was told I couldn't do. I remember being told that I couldn't go abroad to study as I wanted.

People placed these limiting rules on me looking at my background and the circumstances that surrounded me. They were right in a way. They said I couldn't and shouldn't go because no one was doing it or had done it around me.

You can't do it. You are unable to do it. You won't be successful in doing that. You are not the right person to do this. You don't have what it takes to do it. I understood all these because I was from a very disadvantaged background. I had to break these rules to do what I wanted. This was my mindset.

This is how I deal with limiting rules. You can't and won't go abroad for your studies. I can go and I will go abroad for my studies.

You are not the right person to go. I am the right person to go. You don't have what it takes to go. I have what it takes to go. **The desire to go is what I have- this is the foundation, other things will follow.**

How can a person who doesn't understand everything about me tell me what I can't do when I know I can do it? They can't tell me that I don't have what it takes to do what I want to do when I know I have it.

It's okay even if I don't have what it takes at the time I desire to do this particular thing. I can develop myself to have what I need to do what I want. This is unfair. **Are you a progress limiting tool? Are you an enemy of progress?**

Who made you a judge over other people? How do you determine the right and the wrong person when you don't know what a person has inside? The truth is, you don't and you won't know everything about another person. **Some treasures are exclusive to the owners.**

You should be careful. There are gutsy people in this world. You tell them this is your true identity or purpose, and they tell you that you are not the right person to embrace these.

You don't just look at people's outward appearance and jump to conclusions about who they can and can't become: who they should and shouldn't become. True identity, purpose, dreams and desires come from within us. You don't know what the other person has inside them.

It's unfair to discourage people using their outward appearance and the circumstances that surround them. We don't use anything to determine everything.

What they predicted or said about me going abroad for my studies came true. But it doesn't matter. People should be given a chance to do what they want even if they end up failing. Failing is not a crime. It's not the end of life or everything.

It's not even my fault that things can go wrong in life. We need to be given a chance to quench the desperate desires within us. We will come out with valuable experiences and lessons from what everyone calls failure.

Due to some challenges, I came back to my country before I completed school. Guess what people said. **We said it. We told you.** *These are some of the worst statements that can be said to you during your lowest moments.* This was a difficult time. I kept quiet and never proved any point.

Everyone knew it was over with me. But different thinkers and rule breakers don't easily give up. Six years later I went back to school. This time I completed my studies and came back with two certificates.

Breaking these limiting rules is not easy. Successful people go through challenges to become, do or achieve what they want. They have terrible stories to tell. People will place rules on you without hesitation.

I remember telling someone some years ago that I was going to write books and that I had started working on my writing. This was a very educated person. This person looked at me and gave a surprised despising laughter. **What are you writing? What can you write?**

These are some of the encounters that you don't

easily forget. These comments can destroy a person based on who says them. **But a rule breaker with a clear firm pledge is a survivor.** We don't easily give up.

How do you look at a person and jump to conclusions that they can't do what they know they can do? This is unfair. This is the reason I am on a mission to raise a generation of rule breakers who will also give birth to rule breakers. Imagine if I listened to those who believed I couldn't become a writer. *I wouldn't be writing this book.*

Rule breakers don't use other people's situations to determine their outcome.

They understand their individuality and uniqueness.

They understand that they are separate independent beings with the right to think and choose what they want. **I don't determine my outcome by the current situation or the past.** I determine the outcome I want. We don't use other people's situations, failures or outcome to determine ours.

There is a proverb in my language that says, **what ate your mother's child will eat you.** This means that what affected your sibling or family member will affect you. As a different thinker, I don't accept any rule or proverb because it has been there for too long: because it has become a culture that is being observed by everyone.

It's not obvious that what affects my siblings or family members will affect me. We can't be certain. This can happen but may not happen or will not always happen. This can happen but will not happen to everyone or all families in the world.

All your siblings may be under the bondage of poverty but it doesn't mean that some will not break out from this bondage along the journey of life. Breaking free from bondage is not easy but possible.

We should understand the difference between difficult and impossible. Something can be difficult to do or achieve but it doesn't mean that it's impossible to do or achieve.

It doesn't mean that family members will always suffer the same thing to the end. They may all suffer at the beginning but rule breakers in this family will somehow break out. Don't allow these limiting beliefs and rules to stop you from becoming, doing and achieving what you want.

The Bible makes it clear that we are made in the image of God and according to His likeness. God wanted us to be like Him or have some things in common with Him. We are God's most treasured creation and possession on this planet.

The Bible says, God created us for His pleasure.

He is pleased when we become who He meant us to be: when we do and achieve what He meant us to do and achieve. The earth was created for mankind.

God had a plan to have a being made in His image and that's when He decided where this being will live to exercise his God-given power, dominion and authority.

It's very important for us to become, do and achieve what our Creator had in mind when He created us. We can only achieve these when we break all the limiting rules given to us by logic or other people. Make a pledge to be a rule breaker and live as one.

9

BREAKING AND MAKING RULES

Someone made these limiting rules. Someone should break them. The rules were made by human beings, and therefore can and should be broken by human beings. Some people made these limiting rules for the reasons they had.

Other people should also be allowed to make their own rules: relevant rules that work for them. These are not meant to be final rules that should be observed in all generations.

Imagine if some people didn't break some of these limiting rules. Imagine the state of the world if we all obeyed rules like, you can't become, do or achieve it: rules like you don't have what it takes to be, do and achieve what you want.

You wouldn't have fulfilled your dreams, changed that situation, bought that house or built that family. You wouldn't have started that business or project.

We wouldn't have achieved all the great things we have today. The world wouldn't be in this better state. We don't encourage people to break rules without valid reasons.

- We break rules that are not relevant to us: rules that don't work for us; rules that affect us negatively; rules that limit our progress.
- We break rules that hinder us from becoming who we want to be: who we believe we should be or are meant to be.
- We break rules that hinder us from doing and achieving what we want: what we believe we should or are meant to do and achieve.
- We break rules that discourage us from pursuing what we want.
- We break rules that disadvantage the human race.
- We break these rules to replace them with relevant rules that will work for us and the human race.
- We break rules because we are tired of cultures, traditions and practices that destroy instead of

building: rules that destroy people's self-esteem, confidence, strength and courage.

- We break rules with a mission to steal, kill and destroy what concerns us.
- We break rules that destroy people's lives and dreams.
- We break rules that make people feel inadequate to do what they want: rules that make a people to see the positive side of the negative.

We discussed more about the disadvantages of these limiting rules in a part 1. At this stage, I believe we understand the importance of breaking these rules and making our own rules.

We can't all be put inside one container. Some of us will find a way out of this container. We can't all be expected to embrace a general identity when we have our personal identity to embrace. Some of us will break these rules to become what we want to be: what we believe we should be or are meant to be.

We will do all we can to become just this. This is a pledge of a rule breaker. We don't have a place for provisional or makeshift identities. The rule that says everyone should be everyone or be like everyone doesn't work for all of us.

We can't all be forced to do the same things the same way and for the same reasons. Some of us will defy and break these rules. We will have a different mindset, attitude and approach towards things.

We will look at things differently: from a different or fresh angle. We will see things from a different perspective. We will understand and conclude things differently.

We will have courage to do different things from what everyone around us is doing. We will do the same things differently. We will have our reasons for doing things and not doing them.

We will do things when we have to do them not because everyone is doing them at that time. We will do things that are relevant to us: things that work for us.

We shouldn't be forced to be like everyone. You should be like everyone. You should do what everyone does here. You should do things the way everyone does them here. This is how we live here. This is how we do things here.

Excuse me! Says who? For who? For what? Where is it written in the Bible? Our Creator didn't say all these in the Bible. We will break all these rules. We will only become who we should be not what other people want us to be. We will not live under any pressure from anyone.

These rules gave birth to a generation of people

who are in a desperate mission to become like everyone. This destroys the diversity, balance and completion that are meant to be achieved through each of us embracing his or her true identity, purpose, individuality and uniqueness.

> We can't all be forced to being clones, carbon copies, resemblances or imitations of fellow human beings.
>
> The Bible tells us that human beings are made in the image of God and according to His likeness.
>
> I can't afford to be in the image and likeness of a fellow human being. Being the image of God our Creator is enough.

Identity crisis is a tragedy. This pains our Creator. It's an insult to Him. He must be wondering where He went wrong with us. He fails to understand why His image should go through a terrible identity confusion or crisis when He provided a manual to guide us through life. The Holy Bible.

God in His Word says, His people perish from lack of knowledge. We embrace wrong identities because we lack the knowledge of who we should be. This knowledge is found in the Bible.

We go through identity confusion and crisis because we reject our manual for life. Some spaces can't remain vacant. The identity and purpose spaces can't remain vacant.

A person who doesn't know his or her true identity can embrace any identity.

A person who doesn't know his or her true purpose for existence can embrace any purpose.

- When you reject the main thing you will go around following minor things.
- When you don't understand important things in life, you can spend a lifetime chasing less important things.
- When you reject useful things, you will pursue useless things with all your being as if this is the main reason for your creation and existence.
- Following vanity will make you vain. A rule breaker can't afford to settle for these things.

You are what you think or believe you are. See yourself as a helpless human being and you will easily become one. Believe you are just an ordinary being and you will become one. You will be less than a god- the god of the earth you were meant to be by God, your Maker.

We can't all be forced to go to the same direction. Who will go to the north, west or east if we are all forced to go to the south? There will be no diversity, balance and completion in the world if we all go to the south. Different things won't be done or achieved. Different needs won't be met.

We will all embrace the same lifestyle if we are given a rule that says everyone should be like everyone: everyone should go to the south; everyone should do the same thing the same way. We will embrace the same culture, tradition or practice.

We will see the same things in the north. We will do the same things the same way, for the same reasons, at the same time and place. We will or are likely to achieve the same achievement or result, as we are likely to imitate or copy each other. We will end up meeting the needs that have been met already or are currently being met. I hope this makes sense.

As a rule breaker, I pledge to break these rules. I will not live to go where everyone is going. I will go to the north or where I have to go when everyone goes to the south. I will try west if they all go to the east. I will not just join in to go to a particular place because everyone is going there.

I will join or follow people when there is a need for me to do so. I will not go there because everyone is going there: because everyone is expected to go there; because everyone has been going there for centuries. No!

The one size fits all identity or purpose doesn't work

for rule breakers. We can't force everyone to wear size four shoes and expect everyone to be okay with this. We will break this rule.

We will not allow ourselves to be forced to think, believe and see things the same way. We will not allow ourselves to be forced to follow one pattern, routine or procedure.

We can't all be forced to do things the same way or start from the same place. No! Some of us will start things in the middle or from the end. We will do things upside down or the other way around. And we will still achieve what we want.

The life of a different thinker or rule breaker is not an easy one. Breaking rules invites controversy and challenges. **This is the reason many people seek to be buried within crowds or settle in a cult called "the rest".** Support is uncommon for different thinkers and rule breakers.

People have a habit of negatively naming the things they don't understand.

They will conclude that you have a problem if you are different or you do things differently. And it's very true, you have a serious problem. **Your problem is that you want to be who you want to be or believe you should be.** You can't afford to be a different person. You seriously want to do and achieve what you want or believe you should do and achieve.

Breaking rules means that everyone is doing this and you are doing that. They are doing that and you are doing this. Everyone is going to the same direction and you are going to a different direction.

Everyone sees the same thing the same way and you see it differently. People want certain things for the same reasons and you don't want them or you want them for different reasons.

They are all sleeping, and you are awake and seated. They are awake and seated and you are standing. They stand up and you are walking away.

They start walking and you are running. They start their journey and you are about to reach your destination. This is the life of a rule breaker.

People around you spend sleepless nights posting and sharing things on social media but there is a particular thing that gives you sleepless nights: your true purpose. People sleep long hours daily but you spend these long hours working on what you believe to be the main reason for your creation and existence.

They say they are bored because they have nothing to do but you are worried because you feel like you don't have enough time to spread over many responsibilities. They say they don't know what they can do with so much time in their hands and you wish there were more than twenty-four hours in a day.

This is how rule breakers live. They live this way because they broke the rules that are obeyed by other people and have set different rules for themselves. When I sleep few hours because I have to work I am breaking the rule that says I should take things easy and relax like other people. I am breaking this rule to achieve my dream success.

Rule breaking means going against certain traditions or practices. It is said that every human being should sleep eight or more hours every day. But I can use some nights to work. Some nights I can sleep less than eight hours to push my work forward. I can't force myself to sleep because everyone around me is sleeping or is expected to sleep.

When people feel they should always be seated and not live active lives, I choose to live an active healthy life. I take long walks regularly to achieve this. I do this with commitment. Commitment here means that I do this even when I don't feel like doing it. I do it because I need to do it. **I do it as I should not as convenient.**

I won't eat always because everyone around me is eating: because I can eat; because there is food. I will eat when I want or have to eat. I will not be forced to be buried within crowds. I have the right to stand out from crowds.

I have the right to be an individual. I have the right to embrace my individuality and uniqueness. I was made different on purpose, with a purpose and for a purpose.

> Different thinkers or rule breakers are misunderstood most of the times. In most cases, they are unfairly judged and treated. They are always confused to have a higher opinion of themselves: to think they are higher than the highest. They can be seen as rebels.

We shouldn't worry because we understand that there is nothing to gain in embracing these limiting rules. There is everything to gain in breaking these rules and making relevant rules that will help us become the best we can be and do the best we can do.

Breaking these limiting rules means that I will not observe or obey them. I will defy, disregard and reject them. I will challenge and go against them. I will refuse to comply. I will not conform to what these limiting rules want me to conform to.

I will be a barrier breaker. I will break and cross barriers placed before me: barriers that are meant to hinder me from becoming, doing and achieving what I want or should. I will be a line crosser.

I will cross all the lines that stand between who I am now and who I should be. I will cross all the lines and barriers that have hindered other people from embracing their true destinies.

I won't allow any barrier to hinder me from crossing over to my destiny. I have travelled so many miles to reach this barrier. I can't come this far to make this barrier my destination. I have climbed many steps up to be stopped by these barriers.

There are some places that limit most of us. In some cases, we have concluded that these are our destinations. We accept this because it's not easy to break through to the other side. Most people ended here. We found many people here.

We can even justify our stay here because everyone we know seems to have ended here. No one in our family, neighborhood or community has crossed this barrier before. We are okay because everyone around us seems to have achieved the same achievement. *No one is better or lower than anyone.*

I will break records and set my records. I will not be determined by other people's records. As a rule breaker, I don't compare myself with anyone. I don't compete.

This unnecessary competition to me is like putting myself in a race involving cheetahs, eagles, chameleons, horse, tortoise, donkeys and cats.

Competition isn't my thing. I live in my own world, realities and possibilities. I compete or compare myself with myself when I am maximized.

This is because I have discovered who I am as an individual. I understand who I am. I understand how I should be when I am maximized.

I am tirelessly working on becoming the person I have discovered within me, not other people. I don't compete with people. I learn from them to become the best I can be. I don't compete with them or desire to be them. **I learn from them and I use their valuable lessons while keeping my lane.**

Rule breakers break these rules when everyone is on a mission to become everyone or like everyone. I am not the jealous type regardless of what everyone around me is becoming, doing or achieving.

My understanding is that their becoming, doing or achieving that doesn't stop me from becoming who I should be. It doesn't stop me from doing and achieving what I should do and achieve.

I don't see a point in people being jealous of what other people are becoming, doing or achieving.

How does it stop me from becoming, doing and achieving what I want or should?

Jealousy sounds like someone has become all you

wanted to become and there is no identity left for you to embrace.

It sounds like someone has done all the things you wanted to do and there is nothing left for you to do.

It sounds like someone has taken everything you wanted to have and there is nothing left for you to have.

A rule breaker is a different thinker. They don't worry about these minor things. They have serious things to worry about than to worry about what other people are becoming, doing or achieving.

I will not limit myself by what other people are becoming, doing or achieving. I will break the limiting rules, principles and standards of this world to achieve unusual, uncommon, exceptional and extraordinary results in what I do. I will not accept or settle for the average, usual, common or ordinary.

I am a rare breed and a unique brand. I am of a generation of rule breakers, barrier breakers, line crossers, risk takers, pace and record breakers and setters, situation changers, world changers, history changers, makers and directors.

I will not allow my faith, confidence, strength and courage to be destroyed. I will not allow myself to have unnecessary fear for anyone or anything. I will not allow fear to affect my reasoning, judgement and decisions. *I will replace fear with what it steals.*

I can have fear in some cases, but I will not allow myself to be stopped completely by this fear. I will not allow fear to stop me from becoming, doing and achieving what I want.

Courage is the ability to face fear squarely in the eye. On the other hand, courage doesn't always mean the absence of fear. It means that I have fear, but I still do what I want to do in the midst of this fear.

There is this fear that comes with dreams that are bigger than us. Some dreams will bring so much fear. This doesn't mean that something is wrong. **This fear is just a constant reminder to you that you haven't done this before, and therefore should be extra careful when dealing with it.**

Think of the people who fear taking injections. Courage in this case means that you can be uncomfortable, make your body stiff and close your eyes but you still take this injection.

You can linger around that door because you are afraid to enter and talk to the person inside that office. There is nothing wrong with you as long as you end up entering. There is nothing wrong even if your heart pounds terribly. The biggest problem is to allow fear to stop you from entering: to cause you to walk away without entering.

Fear is not the biggest problem here. The biggest problem is to allow this fear to stop you from becoming, doing and achieving what you want.

This understanding of fear and courage doesn't mean that we shouldn't fight to have faith. We just don't want people to condemn themselves because they experienced fear while working on achieving their dream success.

10

DARE TO BREAK THE RULES

In this chapter, you will be encouraged to fearlessly, unapologetically and proudly break the rules that stop you from becoming, doing and achieve what you want or should. You will discover the rules to be broken and how to break them. Ready? Let's go!

As a different thinker and rule breaker, you shouldn't allow other people's opinion, understanding, judgement and interpretation of things to confuse, discourage or destroy you.

You shouldn't allow other people to confuse and discourage you from what you have always believed in. You shouldn't allow other people's point of view to crumbles the structures you have been building for a long time.

Refuse to allow the negative experiences to bring you down and keep you there for too long. Refuse to allow the challenges you encounter to put you down, off and out.

You shouldn't allow situations to dampen your spirits and dash your hopes. Guard your faith, strength, courage, perseverance and enthusiasm jealously and diligently.

Refuse to go away if you are forced to do so against your will.

Dig your heels deeper enough into the ground to stand for what you want.

Strengthen your spirit and character to withstand and survive challenges. You shouldn't allow yourself to be easily overthrown, crushed and defeated. Refuse to be wiped out and to be put to an end by other people's opinions and actions. Develop the ability to withstand and survive challenges.

Refuse to give up in challenges. Refuse to be the type that finds it easier to surrender or admit defeat than to persevere. Stand your ground and refuse to go away if you don't want to go. Stay resolute, dedicated and focused. Hang on there until things stabilize. Move forward during and after a challenge.

Refuse to be controlled by negative feelings and

emotions. Be unshakable, immovable, fearless, strong, and courageous. Have faith, trust, confidence and hope in yourself and ability. Refuse to be contained, controlled or limited by anyone or anything. Refuse to be negatively influenced: deceived, confused or cheated by anyone or anything.

Rule breakers are not man-pleasers. You shouldn't be on a desperate mission to please everyone: to get everyone's attention and approval. Refuse to please everyone at the expense of your life. You shouldn't compromise what you believe in for the fear of other people. Be fearless, unstoppable and unbreakable.

If you don't want to move, don't move even when the rule says you should move. Hold tight to what you are holding even when the rule says you should let go: even when everyone around you is letting go. Recover what you lost.

Rise and proceed after falling. Go back to your original place if the storms of life moved you. When you have fallen and have been wounded along your journey because of the storms and waves of life, the right thing to do is to rise, dust yourself, limp and continue your journey to your destination. Rising after falling is a sign of strength against falling and giving up.

Dig your heels deeper enough into the ground when you are being thrown all over the place by the storms and waves of life. Don't cooperate with being thrown all over the place. Don't allow yourself to easily and fully go with these waves. Determine when to say "enough". Determine how far you will go.

Determine when to stand your ground and refuse to move or be thrown all over the place. Go back to your original place if you were moved by the storms and waves of life. When you have been brought down to a lower place by the storms and waves of life, the right thing for you to do is to climb back to your original place.

You will shame and embarrass the enemy of your progress more by climbing some steps higher than your original place.

Have the courage that will discourage your discourager.

Do to your enemy what he does to you. If he discourages you to give up on what you do, discourage him to give up on you by remaining strong, resolute and focused to the end.

Have some level of power, authority and control over the situations you encounter. Don't allow situations to determine your outcome: what you become; what you do and achieve. Determine your outcome and that of the situation.

Don't allow situations to push you behind

scenes or take the driver's seat in your life.

Don't be discouraged easily. Be determined to become, do or achieve what you want amid challenges. Be dedicated and focused on your resolution even when you don't have the strength and motivation to do so.

Be dedicated to moving forward even when you don't feel like moving an inch.

Pursue what you want even when you feel like retracing your steps.

Get back on track after being knocked out of the race. Don't lose hope if you feel left behind. Take your time but try to speed up. You will reach if you don't give up. Don't remain behind forever. Don't retrace your steps.

Don't quit. Insist, persist and persevere until you become, do and achieve what you want.

If it needs you to crawl to reach your destination or achieve your goal, do it without shame. This is your life.

Don't lose everything you have because you are going through fierce storms and waves of life. Hold on to what you went in there holding. Don't lose good virtues in there.

Hold on to your dream, goal, faith, joy, peace,

determination, strength and courage.

You will need these because the journey of life is not over yet, even when you have won this fight.

Giving Up Explained

- Don't easily give up on what you believe in. Giving up is having an agreement with your enemy that you will take part in working against yourself, life and progress.
- You pledge your loyalty to your enemy that you will team up with him to destroy your life.
- Giving up is suddenly having your enemy's point of view where you used to differ.
- It's seeing more sense in what your enemy is suggesting than the right thing you have always believed in.
- You see a point in going back than forward.
- It's a decision to turn your back on what you have always believed in and valued.
- It's being okay with what disadvantages you.
- It's working for what works against you.
- It's teaming up with your enemy to destroy yourself.
- It's willingly accepting defeat.

Don't let crying stop you from doing what you should do. Do what you have to do in the midst of this crying. There is nothing wrong with crying if it doesn't stop you from doing what you do. Wipe your tears after crying. Rule over embarrassment and shame. Come out to the open after going through embarrassment and shame.

Replace things with what they steal. Replace fear and doubt with faith. Have faith in what initially brought doubt and fear. Start and continue what you want regardless of the challenges in place. Don't procrastinate or quit.

Remain strong when every intention is to make you weak. Be standing even when everything around you wants you to be down.

Go where you have to go even when you are hindered from going there. Keep your focus and attention strong and steady where it is being removed.

Choose to have joy when you are surrounded by opportunities to be sad, stressed and miserable.

Choose to experience peace when everyone around you is in despair. Be composed and calm amid the raging storms and waves of life.

Be who you want to be against the enemy's wish. Become, do or achieve the exact thing the enemy doesn't want you to become, do or achieve. Don't settle for what is being presented to you or forced onto you. Get what you are being denied or what you want.

Be the best of what everyone thought or said you wouldn't become.

Do the best of what everyone thought or said you wouldn't do.

Achieve the best of what everyone thought or said you wouldn't achieve.

Rule over shame and embarrassment. Do what everyone thought you wouldn't do again looking at what you went through. Go back to that good place that everyone thought you wouldn't go back to looking at what happened to you at that place.

Walk around majestically when everyone expects you to be bowing your head because of the terrible embarrassment and shame you went through.

Take your right place even when situations are against you doing so. Fulfil your true purpose without distraction even when everyone around you is doing a different.

Become the best version of yourself even when everyone around you is becoming other people.

- Choose to live again after what you considered life was taken away from you by the challenges of life.
- Pick up and put together the broken and scattered pieces of your life after a breakdown or crisis.
- Put back together the puzzle pieces of your life after they got scattered and mixed up.
- Dare to come back with a bang after a setback or crisis.

Give yourself a yes when you are given a no. You shouldn't accept a no for an answer because there is a possibility for a yes. You shouldn't allow situations to have a final say in your life.

Give yourself another chance when everyone and everything around you deny you this.

Be strong and courageous. Be bold. Be brave. Be fearless. Be immovable, unshakable, unbreakable and unstoppable for you to become, do or achieve what you want. Don't be intimidated by just anything. Don't allow anything that comes your way to destroy you. **Despise most of these challenges.**

Don't allow the shame of what happened to rule over you. Go on with your life as if nothing has happened. **Forgive yourself and give yourself another chance even if you have really messed up.** Don't be too hard on yourself over nothing: over the things you have no control on or the past.

Don't focus on your past. Don't deny yourself the best life you can live now by focusing on the life you have lived.

Don't focus on your failures behind but on the best opportunities ahead of you.

Never give up on yourself even if everyone gives up on you. Believe in yourself fully even if the whole world doesn't believe in you. Trust yourself. Have confidence in yourself. Do these even if you have serious weaknesses: even if you have really messed up. You can work on these. Just give yourself a chance.

Don't give up on what you want regardless of challenges. Be strong. Be tough. Insist and persist for what you want. Persevere and endure challenges. Make a pledge to be a rule breaker and to live as one. Dare to break all the limiting rules for you to become, do and achieve what you should or want.

I AM AFFIRMATIONS: BONUS CHAPTER

These great life-changing affirmations will work wonders for you if you read them, meditate on them and say them loudly to yourself. Do this daily or regularly until the truth gets established in you and becomes a part of you.

Arise and Shine

It's time to arise and live the life you should live or are meant to live: the life you secretly, deeply and desperately want to live, if people or situations were not a challenge to you.

It's time to arise and be who you should be or are

meant to be: the person you secretly, deeply and desperately want to be, if people or situations were not a hindrance to you.

It's time to arise and do what you should do or are meant to do: do that one particular thing that you secretly, deeply and desperately want to do, if people or situations were not a problem to you.

It's time to arise and have what you should have or are meant to have: have that one particular thing that you secretly, deeply and desperately want to have, if people or situations were not a challenge to you.

It's time to arise and shine.

Arise and Shine!

Affirmations

1. **I know who I am**.
2. I am well informed about myself.
3. I am the only one of my kind ever created.
4. I am the only original true version of myself in the entire human race made up of close to 8 billion people.
5. I am different.
6. I am unique.

7. My unique fingerprints say this better.
8. I fearlessly, unapologetically and proudly embrace my true identity and uniqueness.
9. **I know who I am.**
10. I am matchless.
11. I am simply beyond comparison.
12. I am a never to be repeated kind.
13. I am irreplaceable.
14. I am the only true version of myself.
15. I am the first and the last of my kind.
16. I am the beginning and the end of me.
17. I come once in a lifetime.
18. I am a rare species.
19. I fearlessly, unapologetically and proudly embrace my true identity and uniqueness.
20. **I know who I am.**
21. I am the only one of my kind.
22. I am different.
23. I am unique.
24. There has never been a person like me in the past generations.
25. There is no one like me in this generation.

26. There will never be anyone like me in the next generations.
27. I fearlessly, unapologetically and proudly embrace my true identity and uniqueness.
28. **I know who I am.**
29. I am special in every way.
30. I am a very very important person- a VVIP indeed!
31. There is something particular about me.
32. I have certain things that are exclusive to me.
33. I love myself.
34. I love being me.
35. I am an exceptional being.
36. I am incredibly an amazing person.
37. I will not pursue to be a human clone, carbon copy, imitation or resemblance.
38. I will not spend a lifetime buried within crowds.
39. I stand out from crowds.
40. I don't belong to a cult called "the rest".
41. I am a cut above the rest.
42. I fearlessly, unapologetically and proudly embrace my true identity and uniqueness.

43. **I know who I am.**
44. I am not confused.
45. I am not going through identity confusion or crisis.
46. I am not going through a battle of identities.
47. I am not torn apart between identities.
48. I will not embrace a rainbow identity.
49. I was not created and branded with a no identity on my forehead, chest or back.
50. I have a true identity to embrace.
51. I fearlessly, unapologetically and proudly embrace my true identity and uniqueness
52. **I know who I am.**
53. I am not confused.
54. I am not deceived.
55. I am not uninformed about myself.
56. I am not less informed about myself.
57. I am not misinformed about myself.
58. I am well informed about myself.
59. **I know who I am**.
60. I know who I want to be.
61. I know who I should be.

62. I know what I am meant to be.
63. I know what I am capable of becoming.
64. **I know who I am.**
65. I will not be pressured into becoming what I don't want to become.
66. I will not become want other people want me to become.
67. I will not become what everyone is becoming around me.
68. I am not everyone.
69. I will not become what the whole world is becoming.
70. I am not the whole world.
71. I am me, myself and I.
72. I know who I am.
73. I am me, myself and I
74. I will become all and the best I should be or was meant to be.
75. I fearlessly, unapologetically and proudly embrace my true identity and uniqueness.
76. **I know who I am.**
77. I am not confused.
78. I am not a fence rider.

79. I don't live in the middle of the road.
80. I don't live in between lives and opinions.
81. I am well informed about myself
82. I know what I want.
83. I know what I should want.
84. I know how I want it.
85. I know when I want it.
86. I know when I should want it.
87. I know what I don't want.
88. I know what I shouldn't want.
89. I will not allow myself to be pressurized into what I don't want.
90. **I know who I am.**
91. I am not a nobody.
92. I was not created and branded with a no identity on my forehead, chest or back.
93. I am not just an ordinary person, doing ordinary things, having ordinary achievements, living an ordinary life.
94. I am the Creator's original idea and intellectual property.
95. I am the Creator's most treasured creation and possession on this planet.

96. I fearlessly, unapologetically and proudly embrace my true identity and uniqueness.
97. I know who I am.
98. I am not just flesh and blood.
99. I am more than a human being.
100. I am made in the image and likeness of God my Creator.
101. I have the genetic material of God my Maker.
102. I have certain things in common with God, my Maker and Source.
103. Everything gives birth to its kind.
104. I am an offspring of God.
105. I am a god- the god of the earth.
106. I fearlessly, unapologetically and proudly embrace my true identity and uniqueness.
107. I know who I am.
108. I am well informed about myself.
109. I know what I have.
110. I know what I want to have.
111. I know what I should have.
112. I know what I am meant to have.
113. I know what I am capable of having.

114. I know how much I should have

115. I will have all and the best I should have and was meant to have

116. I know who I am.

117. I am not a human clone, carbon copy or imitation of any human being.

118. I am an true original version of myself.

119. I am an individual- separate and unique.

120. I am the first in my world and realities.

121. I have a true identity to embrace.

122. I fearlessly, unapologetically and proudly embrace my true identity and uniqueness.

123. I know who I am.

124. I am not an extra thing.

125. I am not an alternative.

126. I am not a reserve.

127. I am not a substitute.

128. I am not a standby.

129. I am not a second rate.

130. I am not a side thing.

131. I am not another thing.

132. I am not a backup plan.

133. I'm real.

134. I am an original true version of myself.

135. I am the first in my world and realities

136. I have a true identity to embrace

137. I fearlessly, unapologetically and proudly embrace my true identity, individuality and uniqueness.

138. I know who I am.

139. I don't exist to be a follower, a disciple or a fan of everyone, every time and in everything.

140. I don't exist to be a deputy or assistant of everyone, every time and in everything.

141. I am a leader in my own right and way.

142. They lead in their thing and I follow them.

143. I lead in my thing and they follow me. Fair enough!

144. I fearlessly, unapologetically and proudly embrace my true identity, individuality and uniqueness.

145. I know who I am.

146. My Creator wasn't joking or taking chances in creating me and bringing me into this world.

147. I am not a joke.

148. I am not a mistake.

149. I am not a mishap or blunder of some sort.

150. I am not a slip.

151. I didn't slip into this world or life without the knowledge, approval and release of my Creator.

152. I am intentionally meant to be here.

153. I am not an illegal immigrant on earth.

154. I am not a refugee on earth.

155. I am rightfully and lawfully the god and steward of the earth.

156. I know who I am.

157. I am not confused.

158. I know what I am doing.

159. I know what I should do.

160. I know what I want to do.

161. I know what I am meant to do.

162. I know what I am capable of doing.

163. I know when I want to do it.

164. I know how much I should do.

165. I will not allow myself to be pressured into doing what I don't want to do.

166. I will do all and the best I should I should do

or was meant to do.

167. I know who I am.

168. I was not made in passing.

169. I am not a result of a "by the way"

170. I am not a result of "in case" this or that happens or never happen.

171. I was not created with an "if" in mind.

172. I was intentionally created to here and to be me.

173. I know who I am.

174. Nothing about me is a mistake, regardless of how bad and ugly my story or circumstances may be.

175. I was preplanned, predetermined and predestined to be me.

176. I am accurately scheduled.

177. My space is in this generation.

178. I came the right way.

179. I came at the right time.

180. I came at the right place.

181. I came through the right parents, background and situations.

182. I know who I am.

183. I am not a mistake.

184. I can never be a mistake.

185. It doesn't matter how I happened or came into this world.

186. The circumstances that surround my birth or life don't fully determine my true identity and outcome.

187. The situations I have been through or are going through don't change or determine my true identity.

188. They don't determine my outcome in life.

189. They may influence me but I determine who I become.

190. I determine my outcome.

191. I know who I am.

192. People may not fully accept me because of the circumstances that surround my birth.

193. Some people may think I am a terrible mistake or blunder of some sort.

194. Some people may regret my birth and existence.

195. Others may think I am a result of an accident.

196. Others may think I came at the wrong time into this world or into their lives.

197. Some may think I came before my time into this world or into their lives.

198. Others may think I came late into this world or into their lives.

199. Some may think I am a slip into this world because my conception was a surprise to them.

200. Others may think I was not supposed to come completely.

201. I know who I am.

202. My Creator knew me before I was in my mother's womb.

203. He knew me before I was born.

204. He knew me before my parents met.

205. He knew the circumstances I would be born into.

206. I am not a surprise or shock to my Creator.

207. I am His original idea.

208. I am His intellectual property.

209. I am His most treasured creation and possession on this planet.

210. I know who I am.

211. I am well informed about myself.

212. I know where I am going.

213. I know where I want to go.

214. I know where I should go.

215. I know where I am meant to go.

216. I know where I am capable of going.

217. I know where I should reach.

218. I will not allow myself to be pressured to go to any place.

219. I will do all and the best I can to reach where I should reach.

220. I know who I am.

221. I am not an afterthought.

222. I may have been created after the earth was created.

223. But I was planned for before the earth was planned and created.

224. God, my Creator wanted to have a being made in His image and according to His likeness.

225. After God planned to have me, He worked on where this special being in His image and likeness would live.

226. That's when the earth came as an idea.

227. That was when the earth was created.

228. The earth exists because of me and for me.

229. I know who I am.

230. I am well informed about myself.

231. I am a special being.

232. A special meeting was held in heaven concerning me before the earth was created.

233. This was the contents of the meeting according to Genesis 1: 26. God, my Creator said… Let Us make man in Our image and according to Our likeness.

234. Let them have dominion over the fish of the sea, over the birds of the air, and over the cattle, over all the earth and over every creeping thing that creeps on the earth.

235. This is how special and important I am… Made in the image and likeness of the most high God, my Creator and the Creator of the whole creation.

236. This makes me a god.

237. This makes me the god of the earth.

238. I know who I am

239. I fearlessly, unapologetically and proudly embrace my true identity, individuality and uniqueness.

240. I know who I am.

BOOKS BY K.B. ROMAN

1. **Leadership:** Discovering and maximizing your seed of leadership- **Part 1**
2. **Leadership:** Discovering and maximizing your seed of leadership- **Part 2**
3. **You are the god of the earth:** Discovering and embracing your god identity
4. **True Identity:** Discovering and embracing your true identity
5. **Identity Confusion & Crisis:** Identifying and dealing with identity confusion and crisis- **Part 1**
6. **Identity Confusion & Crisis:** Identifying and dealing with identity confusion and crisis- **Part 1**
7. **True Purpose:** Discovering and embracing your true purpose
8. **True Purpose:** Fulfilling and maximizing your true purpose
9. **Uniqueness:** Discovering and embracing your uniqueness
10. **Enemies of Your Uniqueness:** Identifying and dealing with enemies of your uniqueness
11. Wanted: A Different Thinker
12. Wanted: A Way Maker
13. Wanted: A Rule Breaker- **Part 1**
14. Wanted: A Rule Breaker- **Part 2**
15. The Thin Line- **Part 1**
16. The Thin Line- **Part 2**
17. Fallen Not Dead.
18. The Greatest Excuse: I'm Human

THANK YOU!

Wow! You just finished **Wanted: A Rule Breaker- Part 2.** Thank you for trusting me, for sharing your valuable time with my thoughts, for reading and finishing this book.

I love and respect people who finish books. I celebrate you. You are special- a rare species indeed! You deserve a pat on the back. You are cut for greatness. I hope you enjoyed this book.

Get my other books listed above from the below link.

https://www.amazon.com/author/k.b.roman

I will keep sharing valuable information- free books, materials and discounts. Join my email list to benefit from these. Send an email to kbromanbooks@gmail.com with the subject, "JOIN."

Please don't hesitate to share your thoughts with me- concerning this book or anything.

Email to kbromanbooks@gmail.com

Let's interact on my Facebook page. See you inside!

https://web.facebook.com/kbromanauthor/ K.B. ROMAN

May our good God bless and keep you in His name. Go and prosper!

www.ingramcontent.com/pod-product-compliance
Lightning Source LLC
LaVergne TN
LVHW050544160826
845677LV00011B/2173

* 9 7 9 8 5 0 7 0 6 5 9 2 9 *